THAI
Football Tales

Matt Riley

THAI
Football Tales

A Beautiful Madness

First published by Pitch Publishing, 2023

Pitch Publishing
9 Donnington Park,
85 Birdham Road,
Chichester,
West Sussex,
PO20 7AJ
www.pitchpublishing.co.uk
info@pitchpublishing.co.uk

ISBN 978 1 80150 498 0

Typesetting and origination by Pitch Publishing
Printed and bound in India by Thomson Press.

Contents

For Karen. Nothing else matters.

1

Lost Connections: A Love Letter to Thai Football

THAI FOOTBALL is maddening. Breweries and media giants control several clubs, fixing up fixtures where they essentially play themselves, while staccato matches of foul play and time-wasting tomfoolery are overseen by barely competent officials swivelling fearful eyes to powerful shadows in the VIP boxes. Dark money and franchise clubs on wheels roll across the kingdom, leaving forgotten fans to forlornly fall back into the welcoming arms of the English Premier League. It seems a saddening spiral of diminishing returns. And yet. And yet. There is something about Thai football that infects your blood.

I grew up in the 'Democratic Republic' (always run for cover when a country uses the word 'democratic' in its title) of Malawi. The former British colony was allegedly ruled over by the eccentric Doctor Hastings Banda. I say allegedly because, officially born in 1898 – although even by his own admission this was a guess –

it was whispered (it was never a wise policy to say it out loud) that the remarkably sprightly flyswatter-waving murderous dictator was a lookalike. But, looking back on our life in this barely functioning but beautiful country, there is a contradictory magnetic pull that the head repels but the heart embraces.

This leads me nicely to Thai football. Since returning to England I've been building bridges with my local club, Exeter City, using the same networking and leveraging skills that eventually opened Thai football doors. As a lecturer in Business Management at Exeter University I cunningly adapted the course to include the Grecians as a case study and visited the club with my students. Officially it was to give them insight into their forthcoming exam, but I was on a scouting mission of my own. As a fan-owned club, they exist on financial fumes, so I could see plenty of opportunities to help them and develop new revenue streams. This came to nought.

I then contacted the chairman. Over an amenable breakfast in the city centre, I laid out my business strategy. The ideas were well received but they also came to nought. I even offered my services to fill the vacancy of matchday programme editor as a foot in the door, but the trend continued. I came to realise that, in English football, arriviste intruders will be forced out by the weight of history. Whatever I can offer, someone else whose whole family heritage has been steeped in the club's history can do with more authority. In Thailand I was often in a job application cohort of one and, even if other westerners were looking to compete, I had the twin unique selling points of being time-rich and cheap (often free).

I enjoy standing on the Big Bank terrace at St James Park with my friends and often wonder what it is that stops me from enjoying it more (apart from the quality of football that's sometimes on display) and why I am often scanning around the stadium to catch the chairman's eye or see a process in need of my input. Without Thai football, I would not have briefly lifted the stage curtain and seen the mechanics of what went on behind. I would not have the confidence to know how to do the jobs my terrace friends feel awe towards.

Don't get me wrong. My time working in Thai football was financially ruinous and, at my ripe old age, I shouldn't be contemplating another financial meltdown. I have a sensible job and responsibilities. But there is something about the beautiful madness of football in general (and Thai football in particular) that makes people feel, quite simply, more alive. Securing an interview with a former AIA CEO in Bangkok's business district I expected to be squeezed into the amenable Dutchman's busy schedule before being briskly shown the door. Instead, a man whose day was taken up with loss adjustment and asset allocation became animated and emotional about the game he loved. His company was a big sponsor of Thai football at the time and he ended the (far longer than I had expected) meeting with a commitment to sponsor

Thai League Football, the website I was working for at the time.

We met for lunch a few weeks later. Here I was with the CEO of a multibillion-dollar company eating an Italian meal under the Asok BTS train station. He told me how he was being nudged out of the company with a three-year, full-salary package golden parachute if he didn't work for anyone else. At the time, I was bringing in precisely zero to the family coffers. And yet, the feeling I got was that he wished he was doing my job. That's the drug right there. For all the financial sacrifices and time away from the family, I was building my dream, not following it. I always knew that it wouldn't last and we would have to come home one day, which gave each surreal experience an extra potency. In my mind, I imagined during each bizarre experience that this would be my last day in Thailand so that, when that day came, I had taken in every little detail of the time before and stored them away in my mental filing cabinet.

Would I throw in my stable and sensible career to pursue a highly speculative and insecure position if I had my time again? Was I right to avoid the oceans of money to be made as an unlicensed agent of ill repute? It's a yes from me. For my wife and bank manager, well, that's a different story.

2

And So It Begins

IN 2007, life for our family was set fair. We'd been living in Bangkok since the start of the century with challenging and rewarding jobs. I was the head of English for Harrow School Bangkok, which opened under licence from the 'mother school' in north London. My wife worked at Harrow too as the deputy head of a newly built and impressive early years centre. Our two sons were at the school too and enjoying the outdoor life I had always dreamed of for my kids after my experiences growing up in Malawi. We were based on the edge of this polluted city so the air was (slightly) fresher, we lived on the school site in a compact and well-built house to avoid the hellish traffic, and we enjoyed access to the incredible facilities on this greenfield site. And then my mum died. It flipped and emptied me in an instant. Now, 15 years later as the pain that troubled me now warms me, I reflect on Mike Tyson's comment about how, in his 1989 world-title fight against Britain's Frank ('Know what I mean

Harry?') Bruno, he was caught by a left-hook-right-hand combination in the opening round to stagger him for the first time in his professional career. After the fight, despite his fifth-round stoppage victory, Tyson described the punch as similar to being smashed over the head with a plate glass window that disintegrated around him. He would later go on to recall the hugely concussive blow in three other ways, trying to make sense of what he experienced.

Three comments stood out: 'It was like electricity hit me, I saw a white light'; 'You don't even know if you are out or not, you think you might be down but you don't even know'; 'It was like I just walked into a bomb.'

Mum had told us she had a cancer diagnosis but hadn't revealed just how serious it was. The chemo treatment was talked down by her as we sent jokey pictures of us in Thailand wearing the range of hats we had sent her to use when her hair would fall out. What was supposed to be the first session turned out to be her last. It had been stage three and there was no way back.

In the middle of teaching an A level English lesson, I got a text from my dad telling me she had gone. I staggered down to the school offices to ask the combative head's PA if she could book us a flight to London. When she snapped back that it was inconvenient at such short notice, I responded that I would have asked my mother to die at a more opportune moment, but she had chosen the selfish route and expired in her own time frame. Sarcasm is a tool rarely used by Thais, but she certainly spotted it in me and scurried off to make arrangements.

After two weeks in England planning and attending the funeral, I came back unanchored and hollow. I made a plan to drink heavily and run regularly. Starting with a daily bottle of the volatile and faintly evil Thai rum/whiskey/formaldehyde Sangsom, I balanced the pain of running into and staying in the red zone with the numbing effects of the dispiriting spirit. The day was for running and the evenings were for drinking with the six-hour gap between Thailand and home meaning I would be calling my dad late into the night hoping to expand on our mutual support. The plan was always to taper the drinking off, but this process was hastened thanks to mystery Sangsom ingredients. I was starting to wake up in the night with heart palpitations alternated with a perplexingly high pulse. So the drink had to slow, but the running gave me the pain I needed and early morning races around Thailand became therapeutic through their discomfort.

It was also time to upend my career. I had worked my way up to a busy but comfortable job overseeing 16 members of staff. The conveyor belt was there for me to enjoy: a good salary and an annual re-tweak of my role to keep it relevant without the need to reinvent the workday wheel. It was time to jack it all in. One of my main motivations for this was the memory that my mum, despite being a keen sportswoman and a creative soul, had never been given opportunities available to men. Instead, she was thrown into the typing pool's deep end and would spend her career using those restrictive skills while dreaming of exploring her unrequited creativity. Although she could have retired at 60 in 2007, she decided to keep working until 65 to collect more funds to enjoy and explore all those dreams she had put on hold for a lifetime. She died at 64.

My dream was always to work in football, so I decided I would set up my own career using Thai football as a platform and English media as a unique selling point. I had started to create content but the head of marketing and public relations job became available at the school, expanding across Asia. It seemed like the creativity I craved combined with the security of a salary and the perks that my wife also received with her salary packages like housing, education and healthcare.

This role gave me a big boost and I dived into it with gusto. Highlights included spending a week with NASA astronaut Nicholas Patrick, the nearest I will come to sharing time with a genius, and working with the Thai Olympic gold medal winner Somjit Jongjohor. Among the many gobsmacking memories, one stands out about Nick. We had booked him to give a speech to the Foreign Correspondents Club of Thailand and arranged to pick him up at the lobby of the nearby Centara Grand Hotel at Ladprao. Arriving early (as ever) I asked my wife if she thought Nick was an on-the-dot or early guest. I gambled on early and Karen said on time. When the arranged moment arrived, I looked with amazement to see that Nick had come bang on time plus only six seconds. Later, chatting to guests at this stylish venue in the city's Lumphini district, I was recalling how Nick had arrived virtually to the second from his room, down his corridor, into the lift and over to us at the lobby bar. Walking by after I had secured (under duress) his virgin strawberry daiquiri, he addressed me and the group together by saying, 'Check your watch, Matt.' He knew TO THE SECOND how long it would take to meet us. I suppose they don't just choose their astronauts at random after all.

One of my many astonishing interactions with Nick after his visit to Thailand came while I was working for Bangkok club Muang Thong United in February 2010. I was waiting at Singapore's Changi Airport after Muang Thong had been knocked out of the AFC (Asin Football Confederation) Champions League by Singapore Armed Forces. Mooching around the airport concourse with the Thai players trying to kill interminable hours after their cruel defeat to penalties, an email from Nick lit up my phone with an attached photo of his space shuttle preparing to launch three days later for the space shuttle *Endeavour*'s journey to the International Space Station (where Nick would be tasked with completing construction of the Tranquility node). The players and I sat around in bemusement that Nick's supercomputer brain could not only prepare for launch but have the spare mental bandwidth to ping messages and images to people he knew. They probably also thought, 'How does this guy know a NASA astronaut?'

* * *

Every day was different – creative and challenging, but there was still that football itch I needed to scratch, so I decided to moonlight with football, using the 'proper' job as my launchpad and calling card. The Harrow name carried a great deal of weight in well-connected Thai society that football clubs were often owned by. The fact that 23 princes of the highly revered Thai royal family had been educated in Harrow London created even more kudos for me when trying to make connections at the top of the Thai game. I also (as well as myriad failed plans) had some lucky breaks of timing and opportunity. One of them was getting in touch with Manchester United legend Bryan Robson when he was the Thai national coach and inviting him to train at Harrow in return for meeting the students and staff on 28 January 2010 to prepare for an away trip to Iran. Bryan trained his players and, before and after, was generous with his time around the school, meeting the students and popping in to chat with the Harrow Bangkok headmaster Kevin Riley (no relation) and the Harrow UK governors on one of their semi-factfinding/golfing visits. They were suitably impressed when Bryan met them in the head's office and talked through his storied career before being shown around the gorgeous campus and posing in front of the ceremonial Harrow lion at the side of our boating lake that Harrow on the Hill had commissioned.

One of my fellow footballers (I was still playing as captain of Harrow Academicals in the rarified atmosphere of the Bangkok Casuals League), Duncan Kaizer, was a huge Red Devils fan, as was our head chef and football nut Kaew. I managed to invite Bryan to lunch in my office, fed and joined by Kaew and, at the last minute, surprised Duncan by inviting him to join us too. The day seemed to be seamless. Unfortunately, that would prove to be the exception rather than the rule as my work/football-life balance continued to skew from the former and into the latter.

Unfortunately, results didn't improve for the national team (they were to lose that game in Iran 1-0). Later that year, the Thais failed to progress past the group stages of the AFF Suzuki Cup (a competition for the southeast Asian nations often in the shadows of China and the west Asian countries) and Bryan was to leave his post on 8 June the following year due to health concerns. But back on 8 October the previous year in our stadium VIP box, he appreciated a group of friendly faces where he could relax and not worry about stories being made up for the media. He was joined that evening by his highly respected assistant to scout for players when they heard the wine-oiled commotion in and around our box and came over to say hi. Chatting to them over the hubbub, it was clear they were both steeped in football and determined to do things the right way, a philosophy that is often a high-risk one in Thai football. He was also joined by the affable young translator Wasapol Kaewpaluk, who I had met at matches before and would meet periodically during my time in Thai football. Even a decade later, Wasapol continues to work with the national team as a translator. A rare feat of staying power in any football ecosystem, but particularly noteworthy in the choppy waters of Thai football. The tension between my explicit and implicit roles was building every time I was 'out of the office' at a local footballing event looking to gain traction and build networks while the people I was paid to work for were toiling in classrooms or popping into an empty marketing office.

With one of the (at the time) Thai Premier League stadiums just down the road in Army United, there were more chances to sneak out and meet with contacts and foreign visitors. On 7 August 2013 I found out through a club contact that Barcelona were having a behind-closed-doors training session there before breaking the unwritten rule of pre-season friendlies in Asia by spanking the national team 7-1. We'd tried to sneak into the secret training session for Manchester United the month before at Port's PAT Stadium but with no luck. Considering the poor state of the pitch and conditions at the stadium, as well as how far outside the city it was, it showed the power of the Thai Army when important decisions were made. Instead of spending hours snarled in traffic for the glorious kick-around later that day, we decided to lay in wait outside the stadium so the kids could at least get a chance to see and wave at the passing Barcelona superstars.

To help the process of transitioning between the two roles, I invited Kevin Riley ('no relation' was my constant knee-jerk next sentence) and his visiting family to experience the joys of Thai football in the Kor Royal Cup, which opened the new season in the same way as the Charity Shield, matching the league winners against the FA Cup holders. Unfortunately, if you Google 'Kor Royal Cup 2010', an additional word will come up: 'riots'. I had already persuaded the head to sign off on a VIP box at the Thunderdome Stadium (home to our local club Muang Thong United); the ground was also painted in Harrow blue with a large silver lion looking down on the Yamaha home stand behind the 'Ultras' who followed the club home and away. It felt to me that I was getting the best of both worlds with a generous income for a job I could regularly disappear from to attend football events like shirt launches to continue building my base of contacts. I now even had a place to invite people for network events, sweating the school's baht to my advantage.

So, on that typically humid February Bangkok evening, we jumped off the BTS Skytrain at the National Stadium and strolled to Supachalasai Stadium with my two young sons in tow. A decent crowd of 13,000 started to filter in, only 6,000 short of the capacity and, distracted by the excited chatter as I showed my guests to the VIP seats (feeling smugly well connected that I had managed to arrange them through the club), I didn't notice the stadium's malevolent undercurrent. The game started normally as the massed ranks of Thai Port fans filled the stand running the length of the pitch opposite us, with the Muang Thong supporters behind the goal to our left. The game was played during a highly divisive political period in Thailand, which should have given me cause to reflect on what could happen. The following month there would be several protests against the Democrat Party-led government by 'red shirts' supporting ex-Manchester City owner Thaksin Shinawatra who had sold the club for a reported £200m to Abu Dhabi United Group two years earlier. Red shirts were mostly working-class farmers and people who felt disenfranchised by the goings-on of a government they felt didn't represent them. In opposition were the royalist and often privileged yellow shirts that were seen to be heavily influential in the corridors of the parliament and palace. To add to the confusion, every Monday, virtually everyone wore yellow shirts, irrespective of background, to celebrate their love of the highly revered King Bhumibol Adulyadej.

Thai Port fans were based in Khlong Toey, an impoverished and underfunded section of the city only a stone's throw from five-star hotels and conspicuous luxury whose opportunities had been denied to those living in an area originally designed to support low-income families through cheap rents. But, with the exponential and largely unplanned growth of the city in the 1970s, it soon became an area of over 100,000 largely disenfranchised residents. The main low-lying and swampy slum covers around one and a half square kilometres. Many of the tin-roofed homes were on stilts over stagnant, polluted water, and the area is especially prone to flooding during the monsoon season. This neglected community hiding in plain sight was a strong catchment area for the red shirts, and Thai Port fans felt the same grievances were meted out to their financially strapped club (before the recent oceans of money being tipped into it since 2015 by 'Madame Pang' Nualphan Lamsam) on the pitch too.

The club was about to start a dark period of its history when its survival was at risk and relegation seemed the least of their worries. That relegation was also confirmed by Thanom 'The Bomber' Borikut (there is plenty more of him later) who was an official for hire to do the bidding of The Powerful against The Poor. Two years later his blatant cheating would send Thai Port down. It was a game I was at and watched amazed as his decision to award a highly dubious late penalty relegated the Khlong Toey Army following the 2-1 home defeat to Samut Songkhram. Thanom's predicament underscored a wider challenge for creating transparency and trust for the Thai game's custodians. High farce was robbed of its power when the Thai FA decided to force (on pain of a one-year ban) over 100 of its officials to swear before the Emerald Buddha that they would officiate with integrity. Farce became a depressing reality when the referees were led to this auspicious location by Thanom Borikut. This whistle for hire was then, after he promised to change the habits of a career, free to referee with impunity.

This 20 February evening, a strange undercurrent of political tension was starting to simmer. Muang Thong was the elitist, powerfully connected and conspicuously wealthy club that seemed to represent everything the Port fans hated about the elitist 'yellow shirts'. Surprisingly, Muang Thong had two early goals disallowed. Perhaps the officials could sense the broiling atmosphere of threat. A scoreless first half showed my guests the usual clownish behaviour of incompetent officials and play-acting players, but we were enjoying the evening as an example of what makes football in Thailand different. For example, free kicks in Thailand were strangely country-specific. In other leagues, offending players would be required to back away from the impending kick as soon as the official blew. However, in Thailand, the fouling player would often stand millimetres from the ball while angelically enquiring of the referee whether he will be blowing his whistle again any time soon. If the man who was awarded the free kick broke with this bizarre protocol, then it was he who would be given a card. This was something that would make Robbie Fowler, who signed for the club the following year, amazed and confused as he received a yellow for failing to play along with the pantomime. 'Invisible spray' would later start to chip away at this dead time but, of course, this strange preening procession wouldn't stop for free kicks out of the danger zones. It did force games to start inching slowly towards the AFC target of playing for 60 minutes rather than seconds of APT (Actual Playing Time) though.

While the invisible spray may rob players of one of their many timeouts, they will need to source another way of taking a breather. The number of stretcher breaks taken as mortally injured players enter an all-healing portal when carried back out across the touchline has declined noticeably. In part, this is fuelled by fans having less tolerance for the practice and, particularly as an away player being carried past the Thai Port faithful, you leave yourself very vulnerable if you flout your pretend injury right under the noses of a passionate Khlong Toey crowd who are within grabbing distance of the narrow touchline. The wall-to-wall television coverage has also helped as faking players are exposed in HD and ridiculed on social media. The invisible spray is, like all great ideas, brilliant through addressing an emotionally charged conflict point using simplicity. It has been smoothly rolled out across world leagues and, in England, is usually accompanied by a hard-to-fathom cheer from the stands. But, in Thailand, don't expect the same scientific application. In the paranoid pressure cooker of clubs who either run (or are run out of town by) the Thai FA, there will be claims and counterclaim about what officials judge to be strategic free kicks, how they measure out the required 9.1 metres and where the spray is positioned for different teams. It will be another chance to look at the beautiful madness unfolding before us and remark in our best Vulcan tones, 'It's football Jim, but not as we know it.'

Back at the Koy Royal Cup, things were heating up on and off the pitch. With ten minutes to go, Muang Thong were two goals ahead. Leading up to the second, Port defender Pongpipat Kamnuan hotly disputed the awarding of a corner and attempted to convince his fans it came from a handball. This lit the blue touchpaper and by now even I could notice something was deeply worrying as the first flare was lobbed on to the pitch. The moment striker Dagno Siaka bundled the ball in from close range for Muang Thong, missiles started to rain in from the Port fans, with Kamnuan seeming to encourage them to continue. Some of the Port players tried to calm their fans down, but blood was boiling and there was no way back. One of the aspects of Thai character I often talk about back home is how they often fit into the phrase 'beware the anger of a patient man'. Thais will often be incredibly stoic under intense provocation, but when they blow: watch out. It also used to entertain me when fellow *farangs* (westerners) who had size and strength thought they would easily overmatch a Thai in a fight. I always used to say (and was often ignored) not to look at their opponent's physique and stature but stare into their eyes. Some of the smallest men had dark pools of black memories that never left them. They wouldn't access those lurking brutal actions if you showed respect, but a flailing foreigner would be dispatched without a blink or pause for breath like an irritating fly or half-remembered afterthought if they chose confrontation over consideration.

The stadium's flimsy metal barriers, tied together by lengths of plastic string and woefully under-equipped security, were starting to be flexed and tested. Some fans were already breaking through to get at the Muang

Thong supporters who, due to their big numbers, also occupied part of the same stand. Adding to the surreal scene, one of the first men to break down the barrier was wearing a Thai Port shirt and an outrageous blue afro wig. Sensing trouble, some Muang Thong fans headed straight for the exit, but the majority started to walk towards the stand behind the goal, slowly at first and then with building panic as more Port fans breached the useless barriers and untrained security guards were unmotivated to act by the pittance they were being paid. A small group of Muang Thong fans jumped six feet down to the pitch level and tried to move ladders on to the stadium edge so that fellow fans could escape on to the seeming safety of the pitchside running track as the fan movements took on the frenetic energy of a stampede.

Now it was bedlam, with fans fleeing their attackers but running to the stand where only single fans could get out and on to the pitch. A lone Muang Thong fan was seized on by a dozen Port supporters and brutally beaten as the useless police looked on in confused panic. To my left, a shirtless man lay unconscious next to the pitch as his friends buzzed around him looking for the perpetrator. Around 100 fans trying to reach the safety of their fellow supporters behind the goal were penned into the only practical barrier in the stadium, crushed and cornered as sporadic fistfights broke out around them. Their fellow fans tried to kick a hole in from the other side, but there was no way through, and these poor fans were forced to wait like herded sheep for the

Port fans to decide on fight or flight. Pitched battles on the running track broke out with flagpoles and pieces of wood used for weapons.

At the same time, firecrackers and bottles were being thrown on to the field as a prelude to a pitch invasion while furious Thai Port fans attacked fleeing Muang Thong United supporters, players, officials and stadium security. Port fans ripped down the huge Muang Thong flag tied to the stand and paraded it in front of their supporters like some spoil of war as Kirins (Muang Thong's nickname) director Ronnarit Suewacha was standing on the pitch watching in disbelief. It had certainly been a night to remember, for all the wrong reasons and, when we eventually escaped the stadium, I hurriedly bought three T-shirts for me and my sons to change into from our club shirts as Port fans chased us along the Skytrain platform before we dived into a well-timed train home.

Indeed, one of my last tasks representing Harrow was on 9 March, two weeks before the 'traditional pre-season curtain-raiser' of the Kor Royal Cup where I was invited to join the squad for a pre-season photo. They were pushing against an open door if they were trying to beckon me in. On the day of that riotous game, I was asked to host former Arsenal player Steve Morrow at Harrow in his role as Arsenal's international partnerships performance supervisor (that's a long business card). He was impressed with our facilities and I managed to spend the day without asking that question about him and Tony Adams in the 1993

League Cup Final celebration that led to his broken arm. With so much going on, it seemed inevitable that soon I would be able to generate an income from the connections I was establishing. It's always good to dream.

3

The Qatar World Cup Bid

TWO MONTHS later, Muang Thong had the thankless task of playing away in Qatar against Al-Rayyan in the last 16 of the AFC Cup (Asia's Europa/Conference League). To gauge the scale of the mismatch, we didn't have enough players to fill the substitute bench, but they could call on players like former Middlesbrough striker Afonso Alves who had signed from them the previous season. I decided the cost was too much for such an inevitable defeat and stayed in Thailand while my friend and head coach René (more of him later) took the team over there. Astonishingly, we were to take the lead through Teerasil Dangda (one of the kingdom's most successful players during his 11 years at the club) after 17 minutes, but order was restored by Alves with a penalty just before half-time and the next three quarters of an hour saw the Muang Thong defence reenact the Alamo. It was a strange sight watching on television when, at the time, Thai clubs were enjoying huge crowds. Despite the cavernous

Ahmad bin Ali Stadium having a capacity of 40,000, 39,000 of the seats were empty and many of the 1,500 'customers' seemed to have little to no interest in what was going on in front of them. That, it turned out, was to foreshadow many of the Qatar 2022 stadiums which, if they hadn't been filled by foreign workers herded in at the last minute as set fillers, would have had more gaps than Shane MaGowan's front teeth. Somehow, the Thais staggered to the end of normal time and, more incredibly, made it to penalties. But here the Thais had an ace up their sleeve.

Kawin Thamsatchanan (dressed that night from head to toe in white like some Asian superhero) carved out an immense career (on a Thai scale), going on to win 68 caps and playing 20 games in Belgian football with Leicester City feeder club OH Leuven. As stellar as his career had been, it could have been even better if not for an unlucky twist of fate. Later that year, Bryan Robson, after seeing this ultimate professional up close, suggested to Manchester United's goalkeeping coach Eric Steele that he take a look at Kawin. I remember being at a training session in the Thunderdome with Bryan joining us, amazed that Kawin was training for Muang Thong in a Manchester United shirt, something we both felt was a poor decision. We persuaded Kawin to ditch the United shirt and get on with showing what he could do. The plan was to sign him and immediately farm him off to Grasshoppers of Zürich to see how he coped with European conditions. Kawin had already anticipated a possible European adventure by changing his diet and working on his English, but everything would fall to pieces. In a national training session soon after, he collided with fellow Muang Thong player Nattaporn Phanrit and broke his wrist, ruling him out for months and losing his chance of signing for the Red Devils. But, on this May evening, he was to show what made him special and, astonishingly, helped his team to a 4-2 penalty victory. This was incredible enough, but what René heard after the match made the game pale into insignificance.

World Cup bidding had started the year before the match and, after some tyre-kicking countries were filtered out of the process, five remained: Australia, Japan, Qatar, South Korea and the United States. To the naked eye, this list seemed to be made up of four realistic bids and one that was there for profile and promotion by association for the 22-member FIFA Executive Committee to chew over in Zürich on 2 December 2010, seven months after the match. But some of us were armed with some stunning information thanks to our Qatari opponents post-match. So the game had finished and Muang Thong had somehow staggered to victory against these Qataris with money to burn. René started chatting to the home team's management and they shared a story about how, even though they lost the game, they had managed to secure the 2022 World Cup bid, giving René chapter and verse about how they had done so. When René called me, we had different responses. He believed what they had told him but, for me, it sounded like a made-up face-saving exercise from a defeated team. I thought little more about it when I met up with him and the team back in Bangkok.

The season got back under way and, visiting England that summer, I had time to process what I had been told. René is a highly perceptive man who reads people well, so if he feels they were telling the truth, it wouldn't hurt to find out more and see where it leads. My first step took me into the bookies. Putting money on them winning the bid wouldn't hurt. If I lost, then we could afford it, but surely the odds were long and it could pay for our holidays. I went into every high-street betting shop and they all gave me the same information. I could bet on four of the candidates to win the hosting bid, but there was one I couldn't. Qatar. Talking to the people in the shops, they assumed it was because there was no chance of them getting the nod, but when did bookies stop us from bidding on anything that had no chance of success? So, as I had to return to Thailand, a country where it is technically illegal to gamble (i.e. everyone does it but no one admits to doing it), I spoke to some English friends and asked them to pop into the bookies periodically before the December decision and ask if there was a place to bet on Qatar. Still no luck. Just before we left England we took a break from our extended families in Torquay and I spotted a tiny article buried beneath the other sports stories in a national newspaper. Explaining how, thanks to a newly signed marketing agency, they were putting together a highly professional bid that was making them more of a favourite to win the bid, for me, this confirmed that everything René had been told back in May was accurate.

To this day, it turns my stomach to see some of the people we were told had been packaged, bought and sold preening on the Qatar 2022 stage. Some were sacrificed on the media altar but plenty more, if our Qatari whistleblowers are to be believed, still enjoy the spotlight and know that can continue with impunity thanks to the passage of time and the short memories of those having deep pockets filled with cash and gaudy trinkets.

To understand these murky political waters, we need to know the big fish swimming in them. For Thailand, step forward disgraced former head of the Thai FA, Worawi Makudi. A legend in his own lunchtime, he was a member of the FIFA Council between 1997 and 2015, the year he was suspended by the FIFA Ethics Committee. If you're looked down upon from a moral high ground in the committee that would, until the end of that year, report to Sepp Blatter summed up by the iconic image of fake money showered on him by British comedian Lee Nelson that July, then you have some serious issues in need of attention. In 2016, Makudi was banned by the same committee for five years for 'forgery and falsification' after offering to vote for both sides of the bid as long as each party was offering him the incentives he needed. He was a busy man, not only getting involved in the 2022 process but priming England as part of their disastrous 2018 World

Cup bid that collected two votes from the available 22 (and you can guarantee neither of them were Thai). The price for his vote was a friendly between Thailand and England. You might wonder why on earth England would be interested. A year after Qatar was given the tournament, Lord Triesman exercised his parliamentary privilege to accuse Worawi of demanding TV rights for this game in return for supporting England's later bid. It's easy to get fixated on this five-foot Brylcreem oil slick's machinations, but England were prepared to fly out Premier League stars, and not charge for their time to play a country a century of places below them in the FIFA ranking during a break in the Premier League season. Charity or soft power? As England's bid crumbled to dust and the game was quietly cancelled, I'll leave you to decide.

4

Ladies in Red

FRIDAY, 8 October 2010 was a much more enjoyable footballing memory. Our smart VIP box at the Thunderdome was the venue for a Women Wear Red (the colour of the team) evening. I had been getting some deserved heat from other members of staff who thought, correctly, that I was more focused on football than the job I was being paid for, so I needed to do some internal PR. Despite not being a football fan, my wife kindly agreed to drag a group of fellow schoolteachers along with the promise of free wine and a night out after. Luckily for me, they all had a great time, watching the team take part in a thrilling 3-3 draw with Royal Thai Army that helped the home side close in on a second consecutive Thai Premier League title a fortnight later. It was a great way to spend a Friday night and bought me a bit of breathing space while I decided whether to jump before I was pushed from this sensible job and into the beautiful madness of Thai football. I was a believer in the cliche that if you leap, then a parachute would appear, a philosophy I would have plenty of time to repent at leisure. But, for now, the evening was made even more enjoyable by our unexpected VIP box guests.

Bryan Robson had been the Thai national coach for almost a year and had trained on the Harrow pitches nine months earlier. We were lucky to have some of the best pitches in the city and word soon got around. Newcastle United, when preparing to tour the country in 2004, brought Kenny Shepherd, son of the controversial Freddy, to visit us to consider training the players there before their game against the national team and Steve Morrow was officially checking us out intending to base a Premier League training camp there (nothing came of either). When Bryan started his job, I was head of marketing and public relations at Harrow International School based on the outskirts of Bangkok with a huge greenfield campus and, importantly for Bryan, fantastic pitches and tight security that kept out prying and sniping local journalists. Bryan's reign had started back in November 2009 with a win over Singapore in an Asian Cup qualifying match but two draws and two defeats followed, effectively ending Thailand's Asian Cup campaign. The knives were out and journalists were becoming increasingly obstructive and undermining, so I reached out to him and his assistant Steve Darby to offer them our extensive pitches with a promise that no journalists would get past the guards.

This was a tricky time for me, wondering whether to keep going with my sensible job or try my hand at something new. Around this time I decided to start writing articles on Thai football and try to get them published to establish some sort of profile. One of them, for some reason, I sent off to the *Bangkok Post* and thought no more of it. The next day I was called into the head of secondary's office asking me to explain why my name and Harrow School had been attached to an article published in the paper. In the febrile times of political friction when Yingluck, sister of Thaksin, was not only prime minister of Thailand, but a parent at the school, whose son Pike was a friend of my son, an article that the *Post* chose to title 'A Coup we Could All Use' probably wasn't the best thing to add to the political discourse. This was the article that I cringe to look back on and the consequences it could have caused:

'FAT Busters: let's impose martial law on Thai football.

'As we wake up to another depressing turn of the tortuous Thai political wheel under martial law, denials of a coup, ruled by a government without a leader and the Thai economy shrinking by an alarming 2.1 per cent in the first quarter of this year, maybe it's time to stop complaining about the madness and embrace it in Thai football.

'For years, the ineptitude at the FAT (Football Association of Thailand) elicited dark humour and shoulder shrugging, but what if we took a leaf from the book of Thai politics and stormed the football Bastille? Robert Procureur's recent outburst could start le ballon rolling (and he would be the most qualified for guillotine duties). There is a reservoir of rejected expertise that wants to develop the Thai game which, tapped into, would flood the dark recesses of our beautiful game with light and pulse with creative energy that would be highly attractive to globally minded partners.

'The first stage of the process is to get the biter bit. Tie the FAT up in huge swathes of legal red tape. With every dubious decision, file a complaint directly at its head and lodge the case in Norway. The 16,000km round trip for every minor legal update should cool the heels of the FAT head while we get on with running, not ruining, our game. Instead of the highly divisive two football associations in Indonesia, we should empower the legion of inmates against the wardens of Thai football's madhouse. They currently feel disenfranchised and powerless, knowing that if they showed their heads above the parapet there would be more than a football rolling sadly down the road. When the FAT plant their compliant officials in games, the men in black are invited into the VIP box to watch the game while other impartial and untainted officials lead the line. When fines are collected, we use them to finance grass-roots initiatives and support the women's game that is now within one game of qualifying for the World Cup in Canada no thanks to very little FAT support.

'Instead of being seen as the People's Democratic Republic of Football, we should engage in dialogue with the AFC. FIFA are mired in cronyism and infighting as Blatter sharpens his knives for Platini over the Qatar farce, but our local governors are far more rigorous and open-minded. They have to be, because they oversee a group of countries fighting for worldwide recognition and are too often seen as a backwater and sunny clime for players to retire in. By implementing their key initiatives like Actual Playing Time, having strong Thai representation on their Ethics Committee and opening our football finances to root and branch assessment, Thai football can show how much it has to offer the region. If the game here can go from stronger to the J and K Leagues to vastly inferior in one decade, imagine how quickly it could go the other way with professional stewardship. The game here has so much to offer with (generally) well-behaved and passionate fans, highly skilled players and rapidly improving stadia.

'Our income will come from international sponsors. Recently, Citibank were prepared to underwrite a proposed academy league before this idea, orchestrated by former AIA CEO Ron van Oijen, was firmly rejected. Giving young players meaningful competition in a professionally run league was greeted with a mixture of bemusement and fear by the FAT, especially as eight major TPL teams had already signed up for the scheme. Quite rightly Ron, a man who previously managed a company of 40,000 staff, saw the pointlessness of begging for their support and the plan was shelved. There are plenty of other global brands happy to enter the dynamic and lucrative marketplace of Thai football without needing the strings of political largesse and favour trading. The Thai football market is strong enough for major companies to enter it on economic grounds. AIA drastically downscaled their sponsorship not because they failed to increase market share, but partly due to the non-competitive practices of politicians using clubs as electioneering vehicles. Business partnerships with foreign clubs also have a great deal of merit. Most agreements are fluffily worded love notes from a star-struck Thai club to foreign giants pleading with them to be gentle, but the model of J League team's Yokohama F. Marinos shows an open and refreshingly honest approach. The Japanese giants want the following from their partners Suphanburi FC as set out in their Memorandum of Understanding signed last July: "To provide opportunities for each other to meet sponsors of the partner side. To support each other in the commercial exploitation rights (introduction of sponsors in the partner country)."

'The War Elephant may be sharing the bed with two other clubs, but everyone is clear about the situation and gets what they want. For Yokohama, it was access to Truevisions via the Thai club president Varawut Silpa-archa. In return, they will bring the president of the national Japanese broadcaster NHK over next week for some highly publicised flesh pressing and have tangible results to work on. For SCG Muang Thong United's "strategic partnership" with Atlético Madrid signed four years ago, their bed is extremely crowded with seven other clubs vying for the attention of the Spanish champions: their meaningful connections would take highly capable forensic scientists years to locate.

'So, instead of the reverse alchemy currently transforming potential ASEAN (Association of Southeast Asian Nations) television gold into sawdust, a small group of brave souls can scale the FAT tower, plant a fan flag above the penthouse conference room and dodge the ensuing bullets. Led by our spiritual leader Captain Kirk, his *Star Trek* 'Spectre of the Gun' episode will be boldly emblazoned on our flag as we scamper back down to safety, "I don't think we're going to have any choice ... I know the bullets are unreal, therefore they cannot harm me."'

That exposure of a blueprint for Thai football using the Harrow name went down like the heaviest of lead balloons, but happier memories were always close at hand.

A month after the VIP box evening hosted by my wife in late 2010, I had the chance to meet the touring Leicester City team as they visited the kingdom. Their arrival on 4 October came a fortnight before the Thai consortium had been officially ratified by the Football League to confirm their takeover. The club spent a week in Thailand which involved the usual half-hearted friendly and plenty of flesh pressing and stilted *wais*, but they were far more sensitive to the Thais than a request I was copied into from West Ham, contacting a Thai Premier League club about playing a friendly on 29 July 2013. The angle was that 'Big Sam' wanted to visit Bangkok so they would, I quote, 'throw you a bone' by coming. Reading their demands felt like receiving a free ticket for the World Cup Final before sitting down between Gianni 'today I am a migrant worker' Infantino and Vladimir Putin. West Ham would condescend to a 90-minute kick around in return for a mere US$120,000. Their party of 45 (yes, that 45) would, naturally, need their airfares from London covered as well as five-star rooms for everyone (none of them sharing, mind), while 180 square meals a day were required free of charge. For the game, the Hammers would retain the TV rights to the content produced, but the local promoters had the privilege of paying to air it. If the Thais approached their sponsors for help, they couldn't promote either their kit manufacturer or a beer company, neatly cutting out three of Thai football's biggest underwriters in Grand Sport, Singha Beer and Chang. The Thais couldn't even use the official TPL balls but instead had to use Adidas. For tickets, the Hammers required 130 VIP passes, 50 of which needed to come with catering. The Thai team would also be liable for a site visit by four people from London to inspect their club and, most surprising of all, the Hammers seemed stunned when the Thais invited them to kiss a part of the anatomy usually reserved for sitting on.

Sven-Göran Eriksson had joined Leicester City only a day before their arrival after a pair of puzzling and short stints – as director of football at delusional fantasist club Notts County and three months in charge of the Ivory Coast national team, but these were not to be his strangest episodes. Robert Procureur, who I had met the previous year when he was working for

Muang Thong and became friends with over the years, would move on to be a director at Arsenal's partner club BEC-Tero in 2012 and he managed to persuade the former England boss to join him as technical director for the shortest of short-term contracts, which has been airbrushed from his CV. Impressively for Robert at such a small Thai club, it was the 64-year-old Swede's first job since leaving Leicester the previous October. He signed in September 2012 and left a month later after essentially taking a paid holiday in a job where he rarely even turned up for training. You have to assume that he didn't need the money, but that has never stopped him as he made his way around, until recently, the epicentre of overpaying in the Chinese Super League. The memory that stands out from the tour was the incredible way Sven made you feel that he had your undivided attention. Too often, powerful people are talking at you while scanning the horizon for better opportunities. But Sven made you feel that what you said mattered to him. He had a magnetic charisma that could well have been the reason for his long list of bedroom conquests over the years. He, again unusually, always gave the impression that he had time to spare. On reflection, that was probably because he did. He was not a man for being manoeuvred around in search of social upselling.

5

Time is Money: How Matchdays Bridge the Financial Divide

BEING RICH and powerful has its perks, apparently. Those annoying little details like queuing for match tickets or finding yourself in a roofless grandstand seconds before the heavens open are finessed away by minions. But there is a price to pay. Your time is a currency to be used on purposeful conversations that demand positive outcomes, not just spending the time of day. That is fine if football is just another business influence point for you, but if you're a fan, then it's not an acceptable return on your investment. I remember former AIA CEO Ron van Oijen's frustration. His company's VIP box at Ron's favourite team SCG (Siam Cement Group) Muang Thong United would be buzzing with business chatter peppered with PA-fed Wikipedia football facts to contextualise rehearsed conversations. Kick-off times were background noise, but Ron would bravely absent himself from the networking frenzy and sit outside with very clear body language showing, for 90 minutes, he was off-limits. Inside, business bar flies supped model-poured free whiskey while occasionally flicking a half-interested eye towards television screens showing the live action five metres away.

But, in contrast, the cash-poor can be time-rich. Fan families arrive six hours before kick-off to lay out picnic mats and home-prepared food for the day ahead. They luxuriate in a slowly unfolding sequence of fellow fans gathering while children play and creosote-flavoured local whiskey is consumed in frightening quantities, without seeming to darken the mood. Time is their currency to spend slowly, and they have far more of it than the monied few. I have to say I envy them. I was at 38 games a year, but I never saw a full match because of all the interruptions caused by note-taking and sending off content. Televised games were the only time I could sit back and enjoy the action, but the habits of constant distraction at live events make it feel strange to simply sit back and watch.

While westerners see entrance costs to Thai football as laughably cheap, Thai Premier League (as it was known then) match tickets starting at less than a pound can still be too much for some fans. This was something the underwriters of Liverpool and Manchester United's 2022 cash drop could have at least given cursory thought to. 'The Red War', as it is promoted in Thailand, is enjoyed by tens of thousands of loyal but often impoverished fans who see watching either of these two global giants as their lifetime Haj.

As Wagecentre.com reports: 'According to Thai statistical agencies and international recruitment agencies, the average salary in Thailand in 2022 is 14,892.27 baht per month or $435.'

So the ticket prices for the game played on 12 July make for some shocking reading if you are not a 'high so' wealthy local. The cheapest tickets to reward those making it through the hellish traffic out to the Rajamangala Stadium were 5,000 baht (£115), which would finance watching 60 Thai League games, but there was an exponential price rise for anyone hoping to get a better seat. The seven ticket categories are topped by a staggering 25,000 baht offering or five months of an average salary to watch a half-hearted knockabout. To add to the disincentive for attendance, the game also came with a ten-point list of restrictions including demanding all fans wear authentic (and incredibly expensive) club shirts. Instead of getting a fake kit from shops around the National Stadium Skytrain for as little as 300 baht (£7), they are expected to shell out around 3,000 baht (£70), although, this being Thailand, laws are often announced with gusto and ignored with impunity. Fans also ran the risk of being barred entry and forfeiting a refund if they showed a temperature of over 37.5C on entry and had to wear a face mask in the mind-bending heat for the entire match. The risks seem way out of kilter with the rewards on offer, especially compared to a local league game.

Instead of spending the money, fan families at Thai games spend the time outside the stadium soaking up the atmosphere by osmosis. There was also a surprisingly large number of people who didn't even go inside. Instead, they watched the game surreally on television screens metres from the stadium with a five-second delay, so that a crowd roar crashed around them for an event they had yet to see 'live'. Cash-poor and time-rich fans often get more out of the occasion, but the Thai game needs both business and pleasure to succeed together. Roy Keane may have famously criticised the Old Trafford, 'prawn sandwich brigade', lamenting: 'I don't think some of the people who come to Old Trafford can spell "football", never mind understand it.'

But, if football and business don't overlap, the word for football spelling bees to wrestle with would be 'irrelevant'.

6

Your Tinglish
Premier League Guide

AS YOU can imagine, there are plenty of huge contrasts between the Thai and English top tiers, but there are also some similarities. For Thai powerhouses Buriram United, their Chang Arena would put them in 12th place for capacity in the English Premier League for the 2022/23 season. Just behind Leeds United and ahead of Southampton, their 32,600 seats may rarely be fully occupied, but the King Power Stadium clone is certainly impressive. However, the centrepiece of Newin Chidchop's racing and hotel complex is a substantial outlier. Most of the other Thai League 1 stadiums are either diminutive and ramshackle or cavernous and largely empty. For the 2021/22 season, Buriram would average 10,000 (less than a third of capacity) with no other club reaching even half of their total. Of course, Covid will have been a factor, but they doubled the second-highest average total the season before too, even with three games played behind closed doors. Pre-pandemic, the 2019/20 season saw far higher numbers, but only three clubs averaged around or over 10,000 fans. But Thai football is more than numbers. To give you a flavour of the clubs in Thailand's top leagues for the 2022/23 season, it's time to introduce two Thai teams and the English clubs they most closely resemble.

* * *

Manchester City, meet Buriram United. Huge fanbase and power, but just can't sustain success on a bigger stage.

Comparing the storied seasons of both these clubs since Abu Dhabi United Group took over from controversial former Thai prime minister Thaksin Shinawatra in August 2008, City have been Premier League champions and League Cup winners six times each, FA Cup winners twice, and have won a hat-trick of Community Shields. For Buriram over the same period, they have won their top league title twice more than City, achieved one more League Cup win and five FA Cups more. But if their domestic strengths are similar, so are their continental weaknesses. Buriram have only reached the round of 16 once in 2018 and the quarter-finals a single time in 2013 under English coach Scott Cooper. Buriram are, like City, caught between two stools on the international stage. Too big and domestically successful for the second-tier AFC Cup, Buriram have only ever entered once way back in 2009. City are fixtures in the UEFA Champions

League but have only reached the final once, in the 2020/21 season.

The two clubs also share the same background of taking over from an underachieving environment. When Newin Chidchop saw the chance to shortcut a route to the top by taking the licence from Bangkok-based Provincial Electricity Authority Football Club in 2010, he put the club on wheels and took it 400km north. For City, finishing ninth the season before the takeover, the only real blip was in their first season in control when they finished a place lower in 2008/09. But fifth the following year remains their last time outside the top four at the time of publication. Buriram have been just as consistent over the same period with a blip in the same season as City when they finished ninth. Since 2008/09, over the following dozen seasons they finished fourth twice, second three times and were champions on seven occasions.

Both clubs have astonishingly powerful owners with unlimited resources but, until they win trophies on the continental stage, they will always feel a sense of an incomplete project.

* * *

Manchester United, meet Port FC. Lots of money, but not much sense.

Despite owner Nualphan Lamsam scattering millions of pounds into a coterie of scattergun signings, the club finished the 2021/22 season in a highly disappointing eighth, an approach United mirrored and with a similarly disappointing sixth-place finish. Since taking over in 2015, 'Madame Pang' has seen 13 coach changes including a stunning four attempts by Jadet Meelarp and a short stint by former Spurs and England legend Gary Stevens. Like their English counterparts, they decided to move for a highly respected coach to try and steady the ship. For United, it was Dutch coach Erik ten Hag and Port brought in former Buriram United and Philippines national coach Scott Cooper. But, although Ten Hag was to survive and thrive, Cooper was dismissed after a victory in November 2022 and only one loss all season due to 'poor results'. Like United's Glazers, there has been little silverware as a return on investment. For Port, the seven-year Pang reign has won one FA Cup in 2019. For United during the same period, they managed an FA Cup win in 2015, a Carabao Cup in 2017 (oddly the owner of that brand is an ageing Thai rock band based in provincial Suphanburi promoting their toxic energy drink) and Europa League the following season.

Unlike United, Port's stadium has one of the smaller capacities with only 8,000 but it is normally full and rocking with passionate fans who see the club as a part of their community, even if that is more geographic than financial these days. Fans inside both stadiums feel a mutual antipathy towards the direction of their clubs. The visceral and always entertaining Port English fanzine *The Sandpit* wrote an article that could easily have come from Old Trafford in February 2022:

'Moving forwards, the club needs to make major changes, and if the club management is unwilling to do so: they should (in my opinion) relinquish control of the club. To think that because you provide the money, that makes you qualified, just doesn't add up, and can no longer be accepted. If I have an electrical problem in my house, I don't play around with the wires until the problem is solved. I'll call in a qualified electrician, so that the job is done properly, and in the long run: it'll be a cost-effective fix too.'

According to the *Manchester Evening News* in May 2022, the Red Devils have decided to make those changes, with 'More significant changes at the club in response to their disastrous season. United are expected to hire another football director, with several staff changes also planned at their Carrington training complex.'

Both clubs have diehard and historical support, who are poorly served by owners forgetting they are mere custodians and shouldn't bend the club's will to their agendas.

7

Strategic Football Alliances

THE FIRST I heard about these Thai-style partnerships was when we first arrived in the kingdom in 2000. A few of my friends were Arsenal fans and they told me that a local club, BEC-Tero, had close connections to them. I immediately assumed this meant friendly matches, player exchanges and regular visits by the Gunners' coach at the time, Arsène Wenger. The reality was a little more whimsical. The weirdest connection was when, in March 2006, Republic of Ireland legend Niall Quinn played a single game for Tero as a nine-minute publicity stunt. The then 39-year-old soon realised the error of his ways after underestimating the sapping heat, made his excuses and left quickly. I remember sitting down with the then aspiring football powerbroker Robert Procureur while he went through photos from the beginning of that season when Tero players briefly trained at Arsenal and 'my friend' (as Robert liked to repeat) Wenger briefly posed for a picture with the Belgian. If this was a partnership, one half was looking lovingly on while the other was eyeing up the exit door.

Now over a decade ago, I look back on a glitzy evening in the company of Atlético Madrid with a mixture of embarrassment and doomed acceptance. On 28 October 2010, plain old Muang Thong United (as they were at the time) were invited to create a 'strategic alliance' with the Spanish powerhouses that would see both clubs share a range of enticingly unstated activities that remain pretty much dormant to this day. Before the signing ceremony at the huge exhibition hall next to the stadium (one of the largest in South East Asia and, of course, largely unserved by any mass transport), I had joined club owner Ravi Lohtong, expecting to be a member of the background. But the man I always warmed to for his direct and no-nonsense approach made his way over to me (scattering his security guards in the process), put his hand on my shoulder and thanked me for coming. I was surprised at how little effort he had made to dress up when he was about to join the Atlético Madrid president on the pitch for a team photo when I realised why he hadn't bothered. When everyone was set, he was beckoned over, but refused. He saw how much he was paying for this 'strategic alliance' and how little he would receive in return. Nothing would change his mind, so the front row was left with a gap and the photo was diplomatically deleted from view forever.

For the evening event in the Impact Muang Thong Thani Exhibition Centre, I can't help looking back on the photo of myself and coach at the time René Desaeyere with the Spanish PR man and wondering if the Spaniard's hands were resting on our backs, or symbolically picking our pockets. The one clear request of the night (stated in startlingly bold terms by the son of Jesús, Miguel Ángel Gil) was the need for cash to finance the Estadio La Peineta, now known as the Metropolitano Stadium, which cost a quarter of a billion euros. The only tangible result of that unconsummated love-in is how part of the project was paid for by the Thais. The towering, extremely affable and startlingly straight-talking Gil made no bones about their web of alliances across the world, spanning China, the UAE, Morocco, Mexico, Brazil and Turkey, all being revenue streams and, I have to confess, I found his approach refreshingly honest. It was also incredible to be sitting with these footballing powerhouses, considering the financially ruinous career path I was failing to plough.

For a while, I scratched around the local football scene with my fellow fan Chris Roche. We would go to pitches around the capital where one game would have three sets of fans, a single drum (that was swapped over to the next fans at half-time) and games would be played in play, pay and leave stadiums that were dilapidated or part of a local park. Those early days were incredibly enjoyable, but also frustrating in equal measure. In a city like Bangkok where the shortest journey could take hours, games would often be relocated or rescheduled with no warning. This, understandably, put me off away games but even clubs like Bangkok United were notorious for moving home matches, meaning a one-hour drive in snarled-up traffic would regularly terminate in pointless and frustrating outcomes. Even more bizarrely, I once got a call from the coach of the team who were winning the TPL at the time, asking when the game was rescheduled. It had started ten minutes ago. The increasing range of information sources only muddied the waters further. This was the detective work for a trip to a Thai game. Official website: check. *Bangkok Post* ch… hold on, that information is different. Find out from thaileaguefootball.com, but that is different on Twitter. So, ask a player who is selected to play in that game. I promise you that for a Muang Thong FA Cup tie against Pattaya that is exactly what I did. We arrived at the Chonburi Stadium; the wrong Chonburi Stadium. The player was very apologetic, but he hadn't been told either.

As there was no authoritative voice from the Thai FA, clubs could reschedule games when and how it suited them. Suspensions, injuries and transfers could be maximised or marginalised by the most powerful clubs. The FA decided to present the following season's fixtures that could not be changed but 'amended'. I wish I was making this up. Someone needed to take a step back and ask a simple question – this was a product, would you buy it?:

'We can offer you a holiday, but we can't tell you where you are going or when you'll get there.'

'Sorry but the film started 30 minutes ago at a cinema two hours away. Your custom is valuable to us. Please come again.'

Of course, even when a game was 'on time', kick-offs remained flexible. AFC matches kicked off with unseemly haste; bang on schedule. In Thailand, once the dignitaries had their feathers publicly stroked, the national anthem was played, the squads huddled, the teams huddled, the individual hugfests began, prayers were said and flower garlands were tied to goals. A game that kicked off less than ten minutes late was unfashionably early. One of the unwritten rules in Thai speeches for big-dog businessmen and politicians is that the more senior you are, the longer you are required to talk so that, however asinine its content, your pre-match ramblings marked your territory as the top of the political food chain while the players slowly seized up on the sidelines as the kick-off time drifted by into the distant past.

There was a certain gallows humour in turning up to a fixture with a handful of other fans who also made the mistake of believing what they heard, but that wore off incredibly quickly and was replaced by the sound of those who wanted to go forward with Thai football starting to shuffle one step back, make their excuses and do something less frustrating instead. For a year or so, it seemed that this would be the lot of Thai football. The national team was a big fish in a South-East Asian small pond but with a barely functioning league that paid players a pittance and provided very little local pride for the fans. The year Mum died, the 2007/08 Thai Premier League was made up of clubs like Thai Honda, Police United and Krung Thai Bank. Hardly teams to get local pulses racing and fan the flames of regional pride. The league was also overwhelmingly Bangkok-based so, like a World Series, it only had relevance to a specific geography.

But things were changing. In the 2008/09 season, northern club Buriram won the title, with Chonburi, a club based 90km south-east of the capital, coming second. I also started going to our local club with 'Rochey'. At the time, Muang Thong United had been promoted from the regional league the previous year and, in the 2008 season would be promoted again, to the top tier. We were oblivious to most of this, seeing visits to the club on our doorstep as a way to fill the hole left by a football-playing time that was rapidly coming to an end thanks to speedy Thai opponents and rock-hard pitches driving mounting injuries. The 'stadium' was a single ancient stand with three sides of open land ten minutes (or an hour in bad traffic) from our house. But, in early 2009, I sensed that something big was starting to happen. On 19 April that year I happened to bump into Robert Procureur, who was a sometime coach and manager of the club. He told me of the connections the club had and of new sponsors being lined up. He also shared their plans for developing the 'stadium' into one of the kingdom's best. I was naive in the ways of football (and Robert) at the time, but this seemed to be the chance I was looking for – to get involved in a brand-new venture that would help me create a new role and share the passion I had for the game in a different environment. But first I had to jump jobs again without a safety net and, this time, rather than have no income, I would be paying costs out in the hope of recouping them. That was not a great financial plan.

Suitably enthused, that summer I flew back to England with the family, determined to leap soon or else miss out on a unique opportunity (on reflection, this sounded like a crypto scammer call to dumb money about to be siphoned off and never seen again). I visited grounds in England like Arsenal's Emirates wearing my Muang Thong shirt and waving their scarf, tried to get items of club merchandise into the National Football Museum (I know) and plotted my path to English media glory based on the fact that ASEAN (Association of Southeast Asian Nations), whose charter had been signed on 15 December the previous year, would soon be a loose alliance of over 600 million citizens (and potential Thai football fans). This would be a great sell for Thai clubs hungry to expand their markets overseas and increase their profile in English-speaking groups at home.

By the end of 2009, Muang Thong had achieved the treble of two consecutive promotions and a Thai Premier League title so it felt like I had backed the right horse in the race of Thai football's inevitable rise. I was starting to write football content for Thailand's expat magazine the *Big Chilli* and would regularly be seen pitchside with club legend Noi (more on him later). On

13 September that year I was even given the pitchside mic to welcome the players, much to the amused bemusement of the rapidly increasing crowd, virtually none of whom understood a word I said. Although my heart was no longer in it, I continued to work at Harrow, supported in my football passion by headmaster Kevin (still no relation) Riley. By the end of the year, I had invited him to our VIP box and, on 2 November, he was welcomed on to the pitch for the trophy presentation ceremony. He could also see that something intoxicating was happening on our doorstep and happily agreed for the club to use our pitches to train on (the club hadn't thought that having a place to train was a top priority; the first of many head-scratching moments in Thai football strategising). The catalyst for my decision to jump jobs came in January 2010. Muang Thong had previously only employed Thai coaches but, with Robert becoming more powerful behind the scenes, he persuaded them to sign up a vastly experienced Belgian whose two-decade playing career was followed by 16 coaching stints across northern Europe and Japan.

He would return to coaching Muang Thong three years later as well as five other clubs and even now, at 75, he is loving life coaching a provincial Bangkok League 2 club in the stunning coastal resort of Hua Hin. We didn't realise just how successful René's career was until we visited him in Belgium in August 2018. He took me to his old club FC Antwerp and, as soon as we arrived outside the stadium, it was obvious that, for fans of a certain vintage, René was a star attraction. He took me up to the modern and sleek VIP lounge before their game with Club Brugge. What I didn't know at the time was that, for club legends like him, there was also a VVIP lounge on the top floor that I would later be smuggled into. The game itself on 19 August was high on physicality but short on finesse. The only real moment of atmosphere came when, after being one down, the home side equalised with six minutes to go and the game would peter out that way. It turned out that René had played for the club almost 200 times and was a highly respected guest in this collection of former players (including French legend Jean-Pierre Papin) and highly intoxicated and star-struck local MPs. But, on that January 2010 morning at the Thunderdome (as Muang Thong's stadium was optimistically called at the time), my 'out of office' experience created a lifelong friendship.

After the press conference, Robert, René and I met up for drinks in the city. We clicked immediately and, late into the night, it felt that we had known each other for years. During his stay, we often went to the now post-Covid closed Penalty Spot on Sukhumvit Road between Soi 27 and 29. Oddly, the banks of televisions showing games had a two-second delay from one wall to the other so, if you were watching the screens over the bar, those who saw the action on the other side would start cheering or jeering at something that had yet to reach you. It was also one of many bars that knew René would join the house band on-stage to sing Eric Clapton's 'Wonderful Tonight', which brings back happy memories each time I hear it.

We would regularly talk late into the night (often through to morning) about his career and the incredible experiences that football had given. Every time I see former Manchester United coach Louis van Gaal, I think about the four years he and René spent playing together for Royal Antwerp (René would stay for four seasons longer than Van Gaal) and the stories of hungover training sessions on freezing Belgian winter mornings and how René, a man not backward in coming forward, feels Van Gaal is the original alpha male. Surprisingly, Van Gaal is only 6ft 1in as he seems to rise much higher even now he is in his 70s and I'm sure when he was kicking behinds and taking names in the Antwerp midfield with René, opposing players trying to navigate their way past those two must have looked to the substitutes' bench with envy. This would be the start of some intoxicating adventures where I seemed to be trying to dress a silverback in a tuxedo. It might help restrain him, but ultimately it was pointless.

The next 12 months were, understandably, a whirlwind. René had a one-month pre-season to assess the squad, get himself settled and then plot a way to retain the trophy the club had won after beating back 'always the bridesmaids' Chonburi. The Sharks would finish runners-up five times in a seven-season period. We based pre-season at the Harrow pitches which worked for me as I could be present (physically at least) in the office before wandering over to the manicured pitches to hear René shout 'Kill him!' to any timid tackling Thai player. This was certainly a mutual culture shock for the coach and coached. By the time the first game arrived of that 2010/11 season, René had the players fit, firing and clear about their roles in the team. The Thai version of the Charity Shield, the Kor Royal Cup (a riotous baptism of fire I mentioned earlier), took place on 20 February where a comfortable 2-0 victory helped René see the building passion (and unsettling undercurrents) for the sport in the kingdom. His two African players (one of whom, Dagno Siaka, is now part of the club's coaching team) scored that day and would be pivotal through the season. Bizarrely, when I was sleepily heading to work in Las Palmas, Gran Canaria, in 2016, a local betting shop that had decided to put a generic photo of a footballer in their window had stumbled on Dagno's image. It briefly woke me from my half-slumber and warmed me with memories of those six surreal years.

Exactly a month later, back in Thailand, the league season got under way and two tight but deserved wins against teams who would finish the season 14th and tenth respectively were important benchmarks for the campaign ahead. The first big test came in week three with an away trip to Thai Port, a club that at the time were the Millwall of Thai football. A resounding 4-1 win for René sent out an important message to the rest of the league that the title would not be relinquished lightly. The fans took to his passionate sideline orchestrating immediately and he built up a great bond of trust with his post-match beers and stilted Thai conversations with them in the ramshackle bar behind the fast-growing stadium. This sequence of wins gave René the chance to make changes in the facilities (the gym was a health hazard) and suggestions for new players. He seemed to be in a strong position to create meaningful change in how the club operated. The word 'seemed' was doing plenty of heavy lifting in that sentence.

Despite losing the next game away at Singha Corporation-owned Bangkok Glass, they went on a nine-match unbeaten run and would only be beaten once more, away at runners-up Buriram (more of that adventure later). Each matchday had a reassuring rhythm for us both. The team hotel was only five minutes from my house, so I would join René and key first-team player Datsakorn Thonglao to meander through stories in the *Bangkok Post* over breakfast and listen to our captain's thoughts about the game ahead. Then it was on to the tactics board for the squad before the players were sent off to snooze and we returned to coffee and small talk.

The season continued with this reassuring rhythm and the title was rarely in doubt. Even though runners-up Buriram had only lost once all season, they had drawn a dozen games, which gave René's team the edge, and the final margin of victory was four points. The biggest challenges that season came with the AFC Cup that, squeezed between games and involving some complex journeys, meant the players and staff were running on fumes by the end of the campaign. Perhaps the biggest disappointment of that season (and maybe the reason why René would be later relieved of his duties) came in the AFC Champions League qualifier in Singapore on 6 February. We took several hundred raucous fans over there and, despite the Jalan Besar Stadium being modern and compact, there were only a sprinkling of home supporters, who seemed more interested in reading their paper than watching the action on the pitch. Virtually none of the Singaporean spectators were wearing club colours, which contrasted hugely with our Red Legion. The game was to finish goalless with the Singaporeans going through on penalties, while the home team would later be knocked out in Group G with only one win from six.

The defeat for Muang Thong gave us six more games for a chance to win in the Europa League of Asian football, the AFC Cup, rather than being pitted against Asia's powerhouses like Suwon Bluewings and Gamba Osaka as the Singaporeans had been. The AFC Cup campaign started with a creditable goalless draw away at South China before home wins against VB Sports Club from the Maldives and Indonesia's Persiwa Wamena. The big challenge came on 7 April when, for their away tie in the Maldives, the staff needed three flights that took over 16 hours. To help some of the staff relax, vice-president Pok (son of the club owner) hired an island with a submarine viewing room. I hadn't gone due to the cost and amount of travel, but I regret not experiencing that to this day. Although the game was safely negotiated with a 3-2 win, the journey home and fixture pile-up were becoming a serious headache. I met up with René and the squad before their next league game and I noticed one of the players who, bringing his breakfast to his mouth, fell asleep mid-spoonful. Despite a home defeat to South China and a draw in Indonesia, we were through to the serious end of proceedings after coming second in our group. Then came that famous night away at high-spending Qataris Al-Rayyan. We were eventually to lose out narrowly to the eventual winners, Syrians Al-Ittihad, in the semi-finals, but it felt like we had arrived on the Asian scene in the club's first journey across the region.

But the next pre-season would be very different. On 7 January 2011 I had arranged to meet René for a welcome-home beer after he had spent pre-season back in Belgium putting together a list of targets and strategies for the upcoming campaign. Before we met, he had an appointment with the club's management to outline his plans ready to address them in more detail during pre-season training. Before he could begin his presentation, the club director told him he had two things to share. The first was that he was to be made Coach of the Year later that day and the other was he was being sacked with immediate effect. I can still see René, this force of nature, walking towards the bar clutching his blue planning file looking like he had been shrunk and shrivelled.

My wife joined us at the glitzy ceremony where news of René's sacking was starting to leak out to an incredulous press who assumed the Coach of the Year would at least get another season. He was the most sanguine of the three of us. My wife and I were furious with the club and how they had treated him, but he had seen it all before and knew there was nothing that could change it. We met up with a friend of René's who was a major VIP box renter of the club (even though he never seemed to use them). He told us he was taking us to his local canteen before the ceremony, which turned out to be the Grand Hyatt Erawan's best restaurant where Karen and I, petrified that we would need to pay for the meals, looked desperately through the menu for the least financially ruinous items. The head chef came out of the kitchen to tell our host that he had baked a cake just for him and that they had imported some salmon from Scotland earlier that day because they knew he was a fan of it. Desperately trying to source an extra line of credit for the potential cost, we could only relax when our host paid the bill for the four of us as if it was of no consequence as we sighed in relief.

After the awkward ceremony (organised by Siam Sport who owned the club René had led to victory and been let go by, just to add another layer of awkwardness) and sacking combo, we finished the evening at Red Sky rooftop bar on the 55th floor of downtown Bangkok's Central (now rebranded Centara) World. Our host was a hugely successful engineer who designed waste management systems for factories across the world, but he did not look like money. Like us, he was appalled at the treatment René had received and ordered the five-star bar's most expensive bottle of champagne to show his solidarity. After an awkward pause, the waiter summoned the maître d', who carefully explained the huge cost of this bottle and whether the order had been made by mistake. Quick as a flash he told them yes, he had made a mistake. He had ordered one bottle when he really meant to order two. The face-off was won. Now we could relax. Life around René was never dull.

8

Pay it Forward: Zesh Rehman

FOR PORTSMOUTH'S under-18 coach Zesh
Rehman, his career has described a satisfying circularity
that included a spell, where I first met him, playing in
Thailand. Zesh was a pathfinder for Asian heritage
British athletes when he became the first to play in
the Premier League, coming on as a substitute for
Fulham at Liverpool on 17 April 2004, a season that
also featured his current club at the top of the Premier
League table.

Zesh signed for Muang Thong on 19 December
2010, two months after the Atlético Madrid 'strategic
alliance' was launched, and spent four weeks
acclimatising to Thai football and René's coaching
culture before making his debut on 30 January 2011,
in the King's Cup against Chonburi. This was one of
many turbulent periods for the club. René had been
sacked three weeks before Zesh's first appearance and
was replaced by the Brazilian Carlos Roberto who
would leave only a month after Zesh's debut to be

replaced by the stern disciplinarian Henrique Calisto. Added to the carnival of coaches, Robbie Fowler had also been signed as a player five months before Zesh's arrival, which caused huge waves of excitement in Thai football, a country with a massive and fervent Liverpool following. Despite all the changes, Zesh would be a steadying ever-present that season, playing 30 times and even scoring once from his central defensive position.

With my connections through René when he was the coach I started to get to know Zesh and was mightily impressed with what I saw. Highly driven and determined to make his mark on the field, he also showed the same qualities off it and wanted to make the most of his time in Thailand to educate himself about a new culture. This was shown the season before arriving in Thailand when, as captain of Bradford City, he was named PFA Player in the Community at the Football League Awards. This sense of vocation fed into the Zesh Rehman Foundation, which he had set up the previous year, and was built on: 'Principles of community engagement and support for young people, mentoring and role modelling, and using his networks within football to open opportunities across all elements of the industry.'

Zesh's platform is vibrant and full of inspiring, empowering projects driven by his determination to use football as a tool to create social change:

'I am acutely aware of the challenges faced by young people from minority communities in this country, and my responsibilities as a role model. I am often asked to comment on, or actively get involved in, the campaign to raise the presence of under-represented groups across all areas of the game, as players, officials, coaches, administrators, within the media, and even at grounds as supporters. It is because of these experiences and responsibilities that I established my foundation.'

After he had settled into the playing rhythms of the season, I invited Zesh to a Harrow Bangkok assembly to talk about the key messages of his project. Training on our pitches, he had seen the sumptuous facilities we enjoyed and anticipated ways to inspire our future leaders of Thai society. His Premier League experience in England caught the students' attention but his key aim was to share his equality, diversity and inclusion message to inspire and shape our students.

The assembly was very well received and we had other plans hatched in his apartment near the club stadium but, unfortunately, Zesh's stay in Thailand would only last for a single season before successful spells at Hong Kong's Kitchee and Pahang in Malaysia. Zesh was one of the very few foreign players I met in Thai football who saw their time there as a platform to drive change rather than the winding down of a career or a chance to showroom their skills for a bigger league. He is someone to keep a watching brief over as, with his undimmed passion and drive for the game, he is highly likely to make as big a mark in England as he did in Asia.

Revisiting this chapter a year after first writing it, I had predicted a footballer's future correctly for one of the first times in history. If only I'd put a tenner on Zesh excelling when I first met him, I'd still be typing this from the Canary Islands. The measure of the man was shown in early 2023 when, as reported by The Athletic's Ali Humayun, Zesh was suddenly thrust into the spotlight when made Portsmouth's coach against Tottenham Hotspur in the FA Cup, just over 18 years after that notable breakthrough as an Asian player when making his first Premier League start – against Spurs. A hasty promotion, after the club sacked the coach and his assistant, brothers Danny and Nicky Cowley, saw Zesh rush back from his holidays to take up the role after impressing in his academy lead professional development phase coach role. At least his business card will be shorter now!

The Spurs game made Zesh the first British-Pakistani senior coach in English professional football and he described it as feeling 'like a full circle moment'.

His career arc showed just what a driven, intelligent and open-minded player can achieve despite all the pushback that an Asian heritage player, coach and official will often receive. There was also a pleasing echo of the doors to Asian opportunity slowly creeping open when Southampton played Nottingham Forest on 4 January 2023. Assistant referee Bhupinder Singh Gill lined up as the first Sikh-Punjabi to be given a Premier League high-profile role, a month after Ashvir Singh Johal became the first Sikh-Punjabi senior coach in the Championship when he joined Wigan Athletic as Kolo Touré's assistant. Zesh had been player-coach at Hong Kong's Southern while working towards his UEFA Pro coaching licence (the first British Asian to receive one). If there is one quote that feels like Zesh's career mission statement, it is this one he shared with The Athletic. Watch out for this boy. He is paying it forward and starting to reap the rewards. 'If you get immersed in the culture, the likelihood is you'll make a smoother transition. Whether that's different weather, different styles of play or different languages. You need to be aware of all that and basically try and adapt as quickly as you can.'

9

Meeting Great People along the Way

Kawin Thamsatchanan

When I worked for Muang Thong United, the players were starting to command higher and higher wages, meaning they could provide for their families and, like many Thais as part of their strong extended families, spend their whole careers in the kingdom to provide for their loved ones. But Kawin was different. Even in the early days, he had a burning desire to test himself on bigger stages. Learning English, making enquiries about foreign clubs and even adapting his diet to a western one in anticipation of the changes he might experience, Kawin was (and remains) fiercely driven. It was only right then that he would be the first person at the club that took up my invitation to interview him for The Full English, the official club YouTube channel.

One of the problems Kawin has had over his career has been that his astonishingly intense training regime pushed his body into the red zone more often than most and his goalkeeping bravery has also put him in harm's way too often. As a result, his career has been regularly punctuated with injuries. The most high-profile was the one when Manchester United came to call, but there have been plenty of hand and wrist breaks or sprains that have kept him out of action and made him a frustrated bystander.

I interviewed him at the stadium pitch side, where he was frank about his frustrations, but also doubly determined to keep on track with his plan of travelling the world of football.

Matt: Welcome back to The Full English with me, Matt Riley. I'm sure you recognise the person here on my left and here are some numbers for him; 27 international caps, his squad number 26, he is 23 years old (much younger than I am). He came to Muang Thong United when he was 18 and he's been at Muang Thong for five years. He's our number one goalkeeper. Kawin Thamsatchanan.

Kawin, it has been a difficult year with injuries, but how have you made some positives from this difficult year?

Kawin: If I think about the injury I got, it would make me feel down. I focus on the future. I think only one day I can come back to playing football. Nothing is impossible.

Matt: Before in your career, you only had one bad injury but that was when you had a chance to go to Manchester United; an injury I think with the national team. Was that a difficult injury because you missed the chance?

Kawin: Yeah. I was unlucky. I talked with [Bryan] Robson already when we finished the tournament at China. That was the Asian Games and I thought after they finished that they will bring me to go to Manchester and in the tournament, I broke my hand and I've been waiting for three months to be ready to come back to play and when I come back he's already gone from the national team.

Matt: When I saw you come off the pitch against TOT with your elbow injury you already looked to me like you were preparing to recover. How do you find the strength in your mind? Is this something from your mother or your father or something from your belief in Buddhism?

Kawin: The moment I injured my elbow, the first thing I think about was my mum and my dad. I care about him, I care about them and I'm really sad about that. But I think the thing. I broke my leg and that was the worst thing.

Kawin's bad luck with injuries carries on to this day but, rather than suffering the damage he accidentally inflicted it on his club owner, women and men's national team coach Nualphan 'Madame Pang' Lamsam. Accidentally elbowing her in the face before a match in May 2022, the press coverage for this highly powerful person was on a par with an attempted assassination for someone who ended up being diagnosed with some bruising and discomfort. Not a great career move.

Teco

Stefano 'Teco' Cugurra is a rare breed of coach: quiet, unassuming and gentle but blessed with tactical insight and an eye for finding the right players to fit his style of play. He and I became good friends, particularly when he was subjected to a deeply unpleasant campaign while in charge of Chiang Rai United that included a huge banner positioned directly behind his dugout with three words in enormous font, 'TECO GET OUT'. Every game he had to draw on his reserves of calm authority, made even more difficult by knowing the banner had been part-financed by a member of the club's board. This campaign was, astonishingly, despite Teco having brought the club up to the top league by finishing third in the Thai Division 1 in his first season. Finishing tenth in his first top-flight season and ninth the following year wasn't enough for some of the fans and club hierarchy and the sound of damning with faint praise after successful runs and an FA Cup semi-final place were finally enough for him, and he decided to take the invited exit door by three successive single season spells with lower-ranking Thai teams before heading for Indonesia to coach Persija Jakarta and Bali United (where he continues to coach now).

Teco had really helped me out when we committed to getting a player signed by another club and suddenly unsigned (I'll explain that surreal saga later). He gave the player time to show his skills with his one-month trial and then went on to sign him and play him 26 times. He knew I had made an honest mistake and been punished for something out of my control. He would mostly choose Brazilian players and staff due to the ease of communication for this man from Rio, but he made an exception here for an English player and I appreciated it. I made sure I flew up there to spend time with him whenever funds allowed and we would meet up and enjoy local or Japanese food, talking mainly about family. At the time he hadn't had children but, like so many Brazilians (and Thais), family is never far from the surface of conversations and he genuinely enjoyed the updates about my two sons. I think these times also helped him decompress from the whispering campaign in a close-knit and small city where a stunning setting couldn't make up for working for people eagerly looking for enough evidence to justify showing you the door.

Top

Varawut Silpa-archa is an anglophile politician whose father had been prime minister, and he now sits in the Thai cabinet as minister of natural resources and environment. Politicians are rarely popular and his dad's term as PM was divisive, to say the least, but I warmed to Top as soon as I met him. He could disarm and overwhelm anyone he met with kindness. It also helped that he could establish himself in a group of foreigners through the cut-glass English he spoke flawlessly. He, like me, was a stickler for being on time (which always impresses me). He loved the fact that his dad would put the clocks in his offices back by ten minutes so people who thought they were being fashionably late had actually arrived on time. For me, after working for a club that didn't seem to trust or value what I was trying to do, it gave me a real boost to be given complete access to Top's club. I would join away games on the team bus and stay in the hotel with players. As the stadium was 100km north of Bangkok, I was also given a club apartment and had a driver to ferry me around. But most importantly, Top trusted me. I would see things in the office that some people would make online capital out of and he knew it would stay between us. Although I was hamstrung by a resentful local media manager below me (for understandable reasons if he had seen my pay compared to his), I could bring guests directly to Top's office before games and, in a strange crossover with Harrow years after I left my job there, he paid to be a platinum sponsor and I went with him to represent the club in Harrow's cavernous sports hall giving a thank-you speech to my former colleagues.

Charyl

Charyl Chappuis was the pin-up boy of Thai football. With a Swiss dad and Thai mum, he managed to blend the best of both these worlds and was a huge female-fan favourite. He could also play. Starting his international career for Switzerland he was part of the Swiss under-17 team that won the 2009 FIFA Under-17 World Cup after beating the host nation Nigeria 1-0 in the final. He was to play in all seven of the tournament's matches.

I had first seen him from a distance when he played for perennial champions Buriram United in the 2013/14 season, but got to know him when he signed for my Suphanburi the following season in a surprise move. What most people didn't know was that a bizarre injury contributed to the transfer. It still makes me wince thinking about it all these years later but, celebrating his goal in the AFC Champions League against Jiangsu Sainty in 2013, he leapt in the air as part of this celebration and landed awkwardly, hyperextending his knee. The official story was broken cartilage, but it was far more serious than that. The injury was so extensive that (kept secret from the media) Top arranged for him to be flown over to Switzerland and have cartilage grown in a lab before being inserted into his damaged knee. The cost must have been astonishing, but Top paid for it all and even flew over with his wife and children to show Charyl his support while he was lying in bed and contemplating a potentially doomed career. Charyl would go on to play 17 times as part of a loan deal with Buriram before signing permanently and playing a further 36 times, after which he moved on to my old club Muang Thong United.

While Charyl was with us at Suphanburi, he made the international switch by playing the first of his 21 games for the Thai national team. This gave us, as a provincial club, a huge profile boost and we all benefitted from more interest generated by local, regional and global media. The peak would come soon after I left the club and country in July 2016. Bizarrely, sitting in my apartment garden in our new home of Las Palmas in the Canary Islands, I was negotiating a short documentary with ESPN and Charyl that would eventually come out in November of that year. Called *Charyl Chappuis – Inspiring Bonding Moments*, it gave me another pang of regret that, leaving Thailand when I had made breakthroughs that could have led to more exciting projects, I was now back to square one trying to sell my ideas to UD Las Palmas who, at the time, were in La Liga. Just like all those years before, doing the work of promoting a club to global English-speaking fanbases was not the problem. Getting paid was. It gives me pleasure to look back on the short documentary about Charyl and feel I helped bring it about, especially as he was, and I am sure remains, a classy individual.

What drew me to Charyl was that, despite his good looks and charm, he didn't follow the groupies' route that was always available. He had a long-term girlfriend in Switzerland at the time and he knew that any hotel assignations would simply be Facebook fodder and lead to him throwing away his more meaningful connection. Up close, the female pursuit was really something. If we were leaving the team coach chatting, he would be pounced on by hundreds of female fans as I was jolted away to make room for one more giddy admirer. But he kept a calm equanimity each time, something that I would not be able to maintain at his age (something I never needed to find out). Maybe I was lucky that Mother Nature dealt me a different hand.

Milan Dević

I first met the Serbian goalkeeper coach when he was working in the most provincial of provinces, Chainat. This dusty and ferociously hot region 200km north of Bangkok was where Chainat Hornbill were based and I was keen to interview him and fellow foreigner Michael Byrne who had signed as a striker. Milan was a relaxed, friendly, committed family man and I enjoyed a couple of days in his company with me sleeping on the floor of the cavernous and largely empty, dark, wooded hotel he was forced to call home. Heading back happy, what I didn't realise was that this friendly, happy-go-lucky character undergoes a Hulk-like transformation as soon as he occupies a touchline. Already physically imposing, he is often the one needing restraint from fellow coaches which, considering the role of a goalkeeper coach is usually the second row back in a dugout, certainly raises the role's profile as fans in stadiums and on TV see him snarling and seething at yet another dubious decision by the officials.

One story sums Milan up. I was telling him about how my friend Rochey had been driving along the highway when someone cut him up. Seething, as he also had his young son Patrick in the car, Rochey gave the other driver the classic one-finger salute. Hardly missing a beat, Rochey's adversary reached down into his glove compartment, took out a gun and pointed it at him. I told this story to Milan, complete with a pregnant pause ready for his shocked response. Instead, he just shrugged his shoulders and said it meant nothing unless he had fired the gun. Then it would have been a slight cause for concern. They breed them tough in Serbia.

Despite his touchline pyrotechnics, Milan has carved out an extended career in Thai football. Remarkably, he has been working there continuously for over a decade and is now at money bags Thai Port with Charyl. He is a highly capable coach, but I can't help wondering if clubs are also afraid to fire him in case they feel the rough end of his Serbian pineapple.

The supporting cast

What also made the matches special was meeting a rich assortment of other characters on a more casual and infrequent basis. My first introduction to them was on the 'happy bus'. Some journeys away were extensive. For us, we sometimes had the option to fly, but our Thai friends often didn't have the funds for that, so Chris 'Rochey' Roche (the original foreign Muang Thong fan) and I joined them. In that 2010 season, a journey away to Buriram gave you more than six hours to wade through the crates of rough Leo beer that were given free by the club. That reminds me of a strange ABV quirk in those early Thai years. Nowadays, Thailand's own Chang beer comes in at a perfectly respectable 5.2 per cent but, when we first came to the kingdom, it packed a much harder (and more erratic) punch. Apparently, it was 6.4 per cent. I say 'apparently' because there was a strange and often disorientating kink lurking in each can. For reasons best known to the brewers, their ability to consistently fill its cans with beer reflecting the strength it said on the label was hit and miss at best, making the real ABV prone to swing wildly from tasty and refreshing cold beverage to pile-driving head scrambler. Many of the clubs sold the consistently strengthened and cheaper Leo around grounds thanks to their sponsorship of the league, but visiting grounds that chose Chang was a disconcerting game of alcohol roulette. Meeting fan friends around the stadium for two or three cans could either set you up nicely for the first-half action or turn the next 45 minutes into a discombobulating and surreal experience akin to a 2am kebab-house visit.

The beer truck

Small in size, but always there (rather like Noi), the beer truck felt like another member of the supporting cast. As our sobriety diminished, we were enveloped in a curious and collegial haze where the lack of a common language was irrelevant as our shared lexicon of experience and purpose was all we needed. Supporting the happy bus was a tiny white beer truck that, somehow, made its way all across the kingdom. Two thirds the size of an old-fashioned milk float, it was covered in Muang Thong United stickers. When visiting clubs where beer was unavailable, the cunning driver would hoist an outsized MT flag from the front side of this toy-sized van and, when scanning the horizon, we could easily spot our next chance to rehydrate before the game, even after hours of intense hydration on the happy bus journey over. Often, at small provincial stadiums, the only food available would be mechanically retrieved meat products smeared in fiery sauces dated through their nuclear half-life, so sticking to a liquid-only diet often seemed the safest course of action. Buying the beer was also a way for us to support the driver's journey to every away game as his profits were reinvested into his petrol bills.

Pipat

Pipat was the linchpin of Muang Thong fans. Looking and acting like a middle-ranking accountant, his calm and friendly manner belied the huge volume of work he did for the club organising these trips, but also charitable campaigns and even running the New Song Committee. Rochey and I were duly informed that one of our drunken suggestions had been approved by this auspicious collective. Ivorian Yaya Soumahoro had been our top scorer the previous season and even scored a glorious goal to confirm the title win. We decided it was time to have his own song, so we put forward a simple ditty that totalled a single word of 'Yaya' to the tune of 'The Animals Went in Two by Two'. A few weeks later, the whole of the choreographed group in the stadium's single stand was singing our song. We felt like proud parents.

I asked Pipat how the fans (many of them had no English) learned the lyrics to songs with slightly more complex combinations than ours. His answer showed the true depth of his dedication. When encountering a new song in English, each row of fans would have a phonetically written Thai version of the words pinned to the shirt of the person in front and Pipat, with his usual quiet diligence, would drill the fans until they had the alien sounds off pat. The sense of pride for him that two *farangs* (the Thai word for westerners) had dived into his world of vocational fandom was wonderful to see and, even when we arrived at away venues steaming drunk and trying to recall our names (Leo was often the aperitif before the main course of rice-based Hong Thong whiskey/rocket fuel/ embalming fluid), he gave off a sense of paternal pride that we had chosen to experience the real life of a Thai fan instead of hopping on to a plane and meeting them at the stadium.

We weren't the only westerners to start going home and away to games. Belgian Paul De Blieck went even more regularly than us. A quiet, friendly, unassuming and hard-drinking fan, he settled into this reassuring rhythm of pre- and post-match beers in the club car park shacks to bookend yet another win for a club that had a huge influence across the league and within the Thai FA. He was often joined by Singaporean Alwin, a gregarious and passionate fan of the club. I interviewed them both when working for the club for my short-lived Muang Thong United English channel three years later. He highlighted how organic growth of the game takes time, but creates more meaningful fan support than those people who have attended matchdays as part of their job description:

'The first time I heard about them was because of one of my employers. He's a fan of Muang Thong and by accident, I saw on the website that they had a big game playing that day so I asked him if he could arrange for tickets and it happened to be against Chonburi, the match that we won 4-1 and it was my first experience with Thai football. What I like about being at Muang Thong is the atmosphere of the stadium. The fans they sing for 90 minutes non-stop cheering their own team and it's changed my life completely actually because now it's almost four years coming to almost every home and away game.'

At every game, there was always a glamorous seamstress who designed a wide range of clothes in the Muang Thong colours. In her early 50s, she was sometimes accompanied by her equally attractive daughter, but always, slightly worryingly, constantly cradling a plastic baby doll that she dressed for the occasion. The contrast between her confident and gregarious nature and this strange addition to her collection was quite disconcerting, even post-Hong Thong whiskey.

Rochey

Our original English fan, Rochey, would always wear the same Preston North End shirt. He had been at Harrow from the very beginning of the project when things looked dicey and the school were housed in a downtown tower block that made Harrow London increasingly twitchy. We played football there together in a tiny field and continued to play when the school moved sites but it was becoming increasingly clear to us both that football was fast transitioning from an activity to a spectator sport. At any game I went to that he couldn't make, I was always called 'Rochey' even though we looked nothing like each other, but it was good to bask in a little of his reflected glory as a fast-growing band of supporters curiously questioned why an English man had committed to their club.

Noi

The biggest fan was the man with the smallest name. Noi (meaning 'little' in Thai) lived, literally, for (and often in) the club. He would sometimes sleep in the stadium, was to become an unspecified member of the support staff's support staff and never missed a club event. He had a personality that lit up the room, and despite being stabbed in the head by a screwdriver-wielding fan at the Kor Royal Cup riots in 2010 made a full recovery and is hopefully being looked after by the club to this day. For a small man he could also drink prodigiously until, with a final can, he would suddenly need to be looked after and tucked up under the bar or around the stadium. There was something achingly appealing about this man, who needed the care and commitment of others to manage each day and his binary life of beer or no beer, food or none, that had a romantic resonance to our western minds drilled into acquisition and accumulation of objects to define our 'progress' through life.

This group of fans enveloped us in a protective bubble where those who could afford it helped pay for other fans to travel or eat, gave generously to local charities and, in times of family crisis for any of them, wouldn't hesitate to divvy out their meagre resources to lend a hand. This wasn't unique to Muang Thong fans but gave us a small insight into how, in Thai culture, everyone in a family unit has a responsibility to take care of their elders or anyone else in need. Humbling.

10

The Full English

SUDDENLY I had a crazy 48 hours ahead of me. On 24 August 2013 I was finally permitted to run an English YouTube channel by the club. I started with an introductory video explaining what I hoped to provide for English-speaking fans. These are some of the key plans I shared (I think you know how it would go):

'Welcome to the Full English: SCG Muang Thong United's English language programme [by this time the club and stadium had been renamed after the romantic-sounding Siam Cement Group]. My name is Matt Riley and I'm going to be telling you all about the workings of the Thai Premier League champions. We're going to be talking to players, coaches, fans and backroom staff to find out the real stories that happen in a Thai Premier League team. If there's anything else you'd like to know, please get in touch with us through our Facebook page or also you can email me directly at Absolutethaifootball@gmail com. SCG Muang Thong United. Ready for the AEC: ready for ASEAN.'

After the channel introduction, things started well. Keen to practise his English, I was given time with the goalkeeper Kawin Thamsatchanan as my first interviewee – shared earlier – and access to visiting coaches and English-speaking backroom staff. I was even able to create English commentary for highlights packages using a 'studio' of a bunk bed covered in sound-dampening duvets while I sweated over my iPhone (air conditioning switched off to minimise background sounds) recording the descriptions. Match previews in and around the stadium made me feel I had momentum and I would start to create weekly filming schedules to embed myself into the rhythms of matchday content creation. Interviewing René when he was given his coach of the month awards and roaming pre-match around the stadiums looking to interview foreign fans gave me a feeling that I had now been validated by the club but, for some reason, the atmosphere would change. I would arrive at the designated times and no one would show up, staff were not made available to me and schedules were ignored. As I became more and more frustrated, it only served to isolate me further and, with the signing of England international and one-hit wonder Jay Bothroyd, made me realise that my time at the club was limited.

Finally, I had a club-approved platform to show everyone that I was a part of Muang Thong United. This was the view from those outside the club, but I always got the feeling that the senior management didn't know what to do with me. This was to be made crystal clear on 8 January 2014 when the club signed Bothroyd. Before the signing, I was made to feel part of the process, meeting up with Jay's agent Sky Andrew for coffee in the 'Red Cafe' (a glorified portacabin in the stadium car park). This made me assume I would be given access to Jay on signing day, a player who had a strong pedigree for Thai football after coming off spells with Cardiff, QPR and Sheffield Wednesday. But, much to my frustration and disappointment, the job was given to a Thai club reporter with faltering English when it came to the pitchside interview. I was standing over their shoulder in the official club staff shirt looking balefully at Jay and trying to work out why they had employed me, only to marginalise and undermine me. It was time to move on, so I started to lay the foundations for a role with my second Thai club. After René's second spell had ended the month before, Scott Cooper, who I had met and got to know when he was Buriram's coach, took over. We got on well and he was very supportive of the work I was trying to do, but he was soon to feel the same frustrations as me before leaving the club only eight weeks after joining, going on to a successful spell as head coach of the Philippines followed by his return to Thailand with the madhouse that is Thai Port FC.

Jay, like Robbie and Roland Linz who I will come to later, was a player signed without a strategy. As the self-styled 'Manchester United of Thailand' (I know), the club felt duty-bound to add big-name players to their squads: a plan that has rarely worked. They did not know how to play to Jay's strengths and his style of play did not always blend with the type of high-speed movement in huge heat combined with 'Thaiving' and simulation. They also seemed to forget that Jay had come off a fallow six months of being a free agent, so he needed to be introduced slowly and blended into the team rather than being thrown in and told to win matches. Jay always seemed to be puzzled at what the plan for him was supposed to be and, after 13 months, made his excuses and left for a highly successful spell in Japan with Júbilo Iwata and then Hokkaido Consadole Sapporo.

It is so hard to understand why I was used so sparingly. Perhaps the biggest issue was trust, but I went out of my way to ensure they knew all confidences on team buses or late-night hotels were kept. I would love to have made it work, especially as they were a top club at the time with annual Asian adventures across the region in the AFC Cup and AFC Champions League. The one area I come back to (that also happened in my second club) was a feeling of resentment from the current media presenter. In both clubs, every opportunity would be taken to deny, delay, deflect or discredit any work I proposed or created. Schedules I had put together were wilfully ignored and the only way I got most of the projects signed off was to go over their heads to the respective presidents which, of course, only created more resentment.

One other factor with the second club I can empathise with was that I was probably paid more than them. At first at Muang Thong, I was given 30,000 baht a month (around £700) but, when I went to Suphanburi, that had increased to 50,000 (around £1,100). Although it felt sneaky, I then started to reach out to my friend Pawin at Bangkok Glass who was also an anglophile like Top and, as part of a family owning a global brand in Singha, understood the value of English content. He responded positively so I let my current president know about the interest and, in response, he upped my pay to 90,000 baht (around £2,000 a month). This meant that not only was I earning far more than some of the staff contracted to long hours in the office when I flitted in for weekends and midweek matches with my driver and club apartment but my wife, who was working as a primary schoolteacher, was putting in long days and evening work for almost the same income. From their point of view (in football if not my house), I can understand the feelings of resentment, even though they must have known I wouldn't be a permanent threat.

They also knew how to put me in my place. On 31 January 2015, I was part of the annual Suphanburi FC shirt reveal at the Robinsons department store on the edge of town. The cavernous central section was put aside for our stage as thousands of local fans came, in curiosity and mostly support. My bright idea was to produce English on-stage commentary for the literally no local English speakers, but it seemed the right thing to do as a way of showing the club's international approach and enlightened outlook in front of our anglophile president. This was a perfect setup for my colleague. Instead of waiting for the main event, he put me on in the graveyard pre-launch section where, as I carefully explained the club's new approach to English content, all I could hear was a chorus of confusion by the onlookers who managed to rob me of any momentum or confidence. By the time Top arrived for the main event, I had been marginalised and embarrassed enough, so reverted to my acceptable role of pet Englishman doing nothing of substance.

In the months before getting a driver, I would use the ridiculously cheap white minivans that buzzed between the provinces and the outskirts of the capital. For only £2 I could sit in air-conditioned comfort as long as I didn't mind a schedule that was essentially 'we go when we are full' and then hemmed it down the highway back to Bangkok. The last time I used their service was 5 June 2014. The reason I can be so specific? The driver on that day was flying down the fast lane with TWO mobile phones perched on the steering wheel. One was for catching up with Thai soap operas and the other made sure he didn't miss anything on social media. Oh, and he had a bone-shaking tic that meant his head and upper body would periodically shake uncontrollably. In a kind of last will and testament way, I wrote on my Facebook timeline that day in what was, on reflection, an understated way:

'The things that go through your mind in a Thai minivan doing 110 K with the driver watching a soap opera on one phone and chatting to his friends on the other...'

Apart from assuming my last few seconds on earth would be as part of a highway bridge, the other memory was that, casting around the vehicle assuming the other passengers would be in the same blind panic as me, I was stunned at how calmly they took a shaking man with two screens driving at breakneck speeds towards almost certain death. As I am typing this, we clearly made it home, but that seemed to be more by luck than design. Astonishingly, we didn't have any near misses either. I can only assume that other traffic recognised the profile of a driver hunched over two small screens in the fast lane and gave him the widest of berths.

11

Thailand's First Live English Commentary

A WEEK before interviewing Kawin, I had what I thought was my big break in Thai football. For the game against Bangkok United on 25 August 2013, I had been invited to provide the first English commentary of a Thai Premier League match on national TV. Remote controls issued for Thai television sets had a button for English soundtracks that were often obsolete, but I dreamed that we could activate this function to provide expats with an English option to press and get a different insight into the Thai games.

When I decided to leave Thailand three years later, plenty of people told me how they fancied doing my job. They saw I had a club apartment and a driver and noticed my travels across Thailand and beyond. What they often didn't take into account was that for the first two years I couldn't even get arrested. Some weekends I would be sitting behind the goals of a game in the pouring rain or, in the case of Army United's running track, my shoes would be stuck to the melting surface and glue an annoying resin to my soles for the rest of my bedraggled evening. One particularly dispiriting event was when, after yet another wayward shot left the ball near me behind the goal, I kicked it back into play, causing my shoe to explode back to its constituent parts. This was also a time of zero income and any payments given were in kind, such as some pitchside advertising space or articles in matchday programmes, neither of which used my skills to pay the bills. Every journey into Bangkok, every coffee with players and coaches was more debt. It wasn't just the money. Kind people would turn up when I asked to meet them, but plenty simply didn't bother to show, so it not only shook my bank balance but tested my faith in what I was trying to do. After all, I had decided to leave a lucrative job. A small number of good people, especially my wife (who lent me her ATM card and PIN), helped me keep soldiering on against seemingly insurmountable odds.

This opportunity, two days after my birthday, seemed a chance to propel myself on to the national stage and forge a path for other English language football content by excellent journalists like Paul 'Scholsey' Murphy. This local derby against Bangkok United was going live in a full stadium (apart from the away end for a club that has never attracted mass support, despite carrying the name of the capital). The game was to be shown on True Sport, the Sky of Thai football, and was the moment when months of cajoling, begging and nagging seemed to have paid off. I couldn't have been more wrong. Let me tell you more.

It was two hours before kick-off. I knew I would make plenty of mistakes as I tried to key into the rhythm and cadences that a match needed, especially one with names on shirts that didn't always correspond to those on the team sheets. The plan was to try to develop a presenting style that avoided the artificially animated tones of so many in the kingdom and, hopefully, would grow into a trusted source of important background to the unfolding action, both for English speakers and Thai ones looking to learn the language. When I arrived at the VIP box designated as the commentary booth, I was immediately relieved that I had only told a small number of people about my plans. As Chonburi's English voice Dale Farrington wrote, this meant I had a smaller number of people to apologise to after the depressing events unfolded. With the players arriving at the stadium, the booth contained one chair and one table. Full stop. Considering the club was owned by the Thai Sky Sports, Siam Sport you could be forgiven for assuming they could lay their hands on plenty of the necessary equipment.

As so often happens in Thai football, I was painfully conflicted. Part of me looked back on the hours of note-taking, preparation and practice with a wave of building anger and frustration. The other part of me, after a dozen years in the kingdom, accepted that I had finally arrived at the sumptuous Thai footballing buffet and the only thing left on offer was a shit sandwich. Not only that, but an explosion of justified rage would solve nothing and further alienate me from the club and its staff.

At this point, the farce moved up a gear. Siam Sport had decided to create an article about this momentous occasion for their pet Englishman but by now the only technology in the room was my iPad and their cameras. Miraculously, in the next half an hour, a brand-new monitor (still in its box), mixing desk, microphone and headphones arrived and were hastily assembled. Yet again in Thai football, I was exhausted by the effort of trying to be organised, fed through the emotional meat grinder and I hadn't even started. But I refocused and, with half an hour to kick-off, I was up and running. The team sheet was handed to me (not in English, of course; that would have been too easy). I had prepared for this and cross-referenced the squad numbers with the lineups to identify who was selected. This gave me a small spike of confidence. The internet was working, the view was perfect and the monitor showing the live feed was really helpful for showing periods of play from the opposite end of the stadium. This was it. Time to make magic happen. To describe what happened next I pass you over to Dale, who kindly used my middle name as an alias to describe yet another knock back in the Thai game.

* * *

The sound of silence: by Dale Farrington

'In the 23 I've been following Thai football, it has been my pleasure to meet many wonderful people; coaches, fans, players, pundits, journalists and administrators. One of the joys of the local game is its accessibility. It's so easy to reach even those at the very top and everyone – by and large – is happy to give you their time. It is a dream scenario for those of us who write about it and an opportunity for the more ambitious to make their mark.

'In the past few years, the number of foreigners watching and reporting on the game has increased dramatically, and this can only be a positive thing. One of the first to get involved in this burgeoning scene was a bloke called "John" (not his real name). "John" wrote for independent websites, established media outlets, and newspapers. His articles were always worth reading. They were well-penned, well-informed, witty and, mostly, very accurate.

'Through his dedication and hard work, he managed to carve out a little niche for himself and eventually ended up working in the marketing department of two big TPL clubs. He was now on the "inside", and he put his knowledge and expertise to good use by raising the profile – and awareness – of first one club, then the other – taking them places they never thought of going. It was no more than he deserved.

'A few years ago, I, along with a friend, ran into "John" before a Chonburi away match in the capital. He was still employed at the first of his two clubs and was his usual friendly self, but he appeared slightly more excited than normal. After a brief chat, he informed us that he had been asked to provide the first-ever English language commentary for a live, televised TPL fixture. A huge honour and landmark.

'The game was scheduled for the following day and he told us how he had been preparing and shared the details of the setup. He would get his very own booth at the stadium, equipped with monitors and a microphone. This was serious stuff and a big breakthrough for the league – and us foreigners. We congratulated him and promised to tune in.

'The next day, word got around on Twitter and, with mounting anticipation, at 6pm we all switched on our TVs, pressed the "Audio" button on our remote controls, chose the "ENG" option and waited for "John's" dulcet tones to guide us through the action. The match had kicked off and the Thai commentators were in full swing, but there was only silence from "our man".

'Tweets were exchanged and suggestions were made as to how we could access the commentary, "Try turning it off and then back on again." "Switch channels and then switch back." "Click on the DD+ button."

'All were tried and all failed. By half-time, most of us had given up and contented ourselves with the usual pundits attempting to describe the action in front of them. It had been a huge disappointment and anti-climax. What had gone wrong?

'A week later, I met "John" at another game. There were no pleasantries this time. I waded straight in with the question that was on everyone's lips: '"What happened? Why didn't you do the commentary?"

'"I did," he replied.

'"No one could hear you," I responded. "We were all trying to find it, but no one could hear you."

'He looked at me. His face was a mixture of betrayal, disappointment and embarrassment. "That's because they didn't turn it on," he said. "I sat in that little room talking to myself for two hours."

'After a brief pause, we both started laughing. Even though he'd been badly let down, "John" could see the funny side and, if he was being honest, it was probably what he had expected to happen.

'Sadly, "John" has now moved away and Thai football – especially the English language coverage – is all the poorer for his absence. I don't think there'll ever be anyone who can match the quality of his writing and levels of enthusiasm. However, for all he contributed to the local scene, I'll always remember the day he thought he was making history, but, in effect, was just talking to himself.'

12

Meet Your Heroes

'SHAW; WILLIAMS prepared to venture down left. There's a great ball played in for Tony Morley. It must be. It is! Peter Withe!'

When Brian Moore uttered those immortal words as Peter Withe shinned home the 67th-minute winner to confirm Aston Villa as European champions against a Rolls-Royce Bayern Munich team in 1982, this 14-year-old would never have thought several decades later, thanks to Thai football, I would get to know Peter, his wife Kathy and son Jason. But, thanks to the beautiful madness of Thai football, that is exactly what happened.

Peter had enjoyed a highly successful spell as Thai national manager, starting two years before we arrived, in 1998. Three years into our stay he would be summarily sacked. Officially it was due to his team failing to get further than the opening round of the ASEAN Football Championship (then known as the Tiger Cup), a tournament in which he had guided the kingdom to victory in 2000 and 2002. But, as always, there was plenty of politics behind the scenes and local jealousy that a foreigner could come in and impose a different (and highly effective) style on the team. A classic example of how the tide was turning came after an Olympic qualifying game against the United Arab Emirates in September 2003. The Thais were brutally exposed and defeated 4-1, effectively ending their dreams of joining the 2004 Games in Greece, a fate sealed after the second leg in Bangkok a week later ended in a 1-1 draw. Peter chose to wear shorts and was banned from the touchline by the Thai FA. The president of the Football Association of Thailand (FAT), Vijitr Getkaew, admonished him for wearing shorts, not a suit. Rather than a warning about standards, this was an invitation to leave; one that Peter took up and he was to guide Indonesia to success in the 2004 Tiger Cup as runners-up.

As Peter shared with *The Observer*'s Lee Honeyball in February 2005:

'It was never about the shorts. It was because we'd lost to the United Arab Emirates and failed to qualify for the Olympics. He made an issue where there wasn't one. I told him they were my work clothes and that I like to go on the pitch before a game to take the warm-up. The temperature is normally in the 90s; why should I wear a pair of trousers?'

I first met Peter in 2013 when he was back coaching with a coastal club, 200km south of the capital, called PTT Rayong. Flush with oceans of cash from the state-owned oil and gas company but mired in dark politics, it only lasted for one turbulent season that finished with 17th place and relegation. Peter then went on to coach for a season at a provincial club, an hour's drive west of Bangkok, called Nakhon Pathom United, where he guided them to their highest-ever position of fifth in the kingdom's top tier before making way for his son Jason, who also stayed for a single season. I tried to help Peter find Thai clubs to manage but, like René, his strident approach and perception in the game of being aggressive and confrontational meant clubs rarely followed up on my calls. When you have so many clubs controlled by powerful politicians, the last thing many of them want is a foreign coach who demands autonomy and time. The first is threatening and the second blocks the owner from hailing the next new face from the coaching taxi rank, so is rarely offered and, even when it works for national coach Mano Pölking who guided Bangkok United for six successful seasons, is seen as an outlier rather than a case study in success.

The abiding memory of my time getting to know the Withes was sitting in Terminal 21, one of downtown Bangkok's many trendy shopping malls, on 4 January 2015 with Peter and Gary Stevens, who was also looking for clubs to manage and would go on to have fleeting spells with Thai Port and Army United. The Villa Supporters' Club of Thailand (which I was a member of) brought in a delegation to present Peter with their official shirt with his name on the back. Rather like Spinal Tap's manager describing how opening for a puppet show simply meant 'their appeal is becoming more selective', we were a small but mighty group. Sitting there in Coffee World wearing my white European Cup Final shirt my mum had bought me just before she died and watching the interaction with two former English football legends gave me huge satisfaction and a glowing memory that warms me to this day. Of course, it led to nothing tangible, but I was becoming comfortable with that by then.

13

Not So Corporate Hospitality

A WEEK after my Kawin interview, I invited a group of Harrow students for a match on the pitch before being the mascots for the game against Chonburi. I had a plan, but plenty of people at the club didn't have a clue. There were three key disasters. The first came when I ushered the Harrow parents up to the expensive seats to see the warm-up game. The club had not booked a VIP box in a game that, in those days, was always sold out. So, instead of giving our Harrow parents an exclusive experience where they could see a club they might sponsor, join or buy boxes from, we ended up trespassing in someone else's box while the owners sat confused at this group of foreigners invading the place they had paid handsomely for. The second disaster was the huge tropical storm that meant the main game would be barely playable and the pre-match one cancelled. I notched my hat-trick when it turned out that the youngest Harrow players were unavailable that day, so we would have to use an older age group.

As the children walked on before kick-off with a club in Chonburi known for their speed and small stature, it became obvious that they would tower over their assigned player and, when the pre-match footage scanned the teams, all that could be seen was the Harrow teenagers and the odd snippet of a Chonburi blue shirt behind.

The match was reasonably entertaining for our guests when current Muang Thong coach Mario Gjurovski put the home side ahead, before the game ended in a 1-1 draw. Luckily for our visitors, he chose not to celebrate the same way he had four months earlier. Now a YouTube hit, when scoring against the team just down the road, TOT (strangely nicknamed 'The Hello Boys') celebrated by removing his shorts and putting them on his head to be rewarded with a red card and online infamy. Through the Harrow evening, I was steaming angry that the club had put me in this position but, of course, when I next met them, I was forced to play the *greng jai* (a complex Thai social norm I talk about later) game and apologise for my mistakes in planning and preparing the schedule. Oh, and they hadn't even prepared tickets for our guests so I had to smuggle 20 adults into a full stadium. Grasping at straws, at least in Thailand this is a perfectly realistic plan, when in most countries it would signal the end of our evening.

That level of organisation was on stark display the following month. I strolled down to the stadium ready to watch training but was surprised to see the team coach in the car park. As I went to investigate, I was chivvied onboard and told we were off for a weekend's training camp in a place called Saraburi, 100km away, and was asked why I had turned up late. The reason? No one had bothered to tell me. So there I was with only the clothes on my back and nothing more than my iPhone. As I interviewed sponsors who were promoting the club's Kick and Share campaign after training in Saraburi, I grew more and more conscious of having no change of clothes in the sweltering conditions. After watching and commentating on the training session, I decided I needed to hand-wash my clothes and hang them on the balcony to use the hot conditions as a tumble dryer. What I hadn't factored in was a building late-afternoon storm that meant my clothes had blown off and disappeared into the swimming pool below. So, appearing to be ready for a swim with my room towel, I strolled down to chat with the lounging players, unknown to them stark naked underneath as I fished my clothes out of the pool. The training centre was in the middle of nowhere so there was nothing for it but to put the wet clothes back on and marinate in them for the rest of the evening.

This reminds me of another training-camp disaster when I worked for Suphanburi. There is a beautiful national park called Khao Yai three hours north of Bangkok where I had the privilege of staying with the Thai Olympic boxing team as they prepared for the 2008 Olympics and where Somjit Jongjohor was to win a gold medal. The clean air, cooler temperatures and simpler life make it a magnet for people looking to escape the strangulating heat of Bangkok. On 12 January 2015, thanks to the friendship of Muang Thong vice-president Pok and Suphanburi's owner Top, we were given use of the Kirin Sports Centre. First impressions were positive as we rolled up in the team coach. Separate huts for the players, a good training surface and places to meet, eat and relax, with a social room as part of the complex.

The only things missing were – well, everything. In this isolated place, we hadn't been told there would be no food or water, bedding, cleaners, or anyone to help us make everything work. The driver jumped back on the bus and tried to empty any 7-11 (Thailand's favourite and super-abundant corner shop) he came across, but this just wasn't going to work and, when Top found out about what had happened, we were summarily put back on the coach and returned to Suphanburi. I had the bright idea of buying a GoPro camera with a harness, putting the players in it and using it to create content of the training to give a unique view of the game, especially when it was used by the goalkeepers. Away from the pressure of in-season training, this seemed like the perfect time to try new things out with building fitness before the season became the key goal. I was only able to make one video before we left. The bank account took another beating.

14

The Referee's a Bomber

KNOWN IN the Thai press as 'Bomber Man', and to his friends as just plain 'Bomber', Thanom Borikut sounded like he came from the pages of a badly written crime novel. In 2009 he confessed to planting a bomb and killing his boss for restricting his development as a FIFA referee abroad. He had hoped to represent Asia at the 2010 World Cup, but when it was clear he wouldn't be selected, for reasons known only to him, he thought that murder was the best way to solve this pesky impasse. It was a clear case where the evidence was irrefutable and he wasn't denying it. An open and shut case, this was going to be the end of him as a referee and the beginning of a decades-long sentence. Then, to most people's amazement, he was only given five years for murder. Stunningly, he even appealed against it and was released on bail in short order to officiate domestic matches. The murder case against him went away, despite a stunned Metropolitan police chief Kamronwit Thoopkrachang, describing how:

'I arrested him in that case in 2009. I thought I did a good case but I don't know how he walked free.'

For most people, the premeditated murder of your boss would put a definite kink in your career development: but for Bomber Man it was only the end of the beginning. Let me tell you more.

Three short years after his conviction, he was back to officiating and was a man pursuing a plan. In a Thai Premier League match between Chiang Rai United and lowly Wuachon United, he awarded Chiang Rai a controversial penalty before sending off three Wuachon players in the final ten minutes when the underdogs were unexpectedly ahead. His actions managed to salvage a draw for the home team, but the focus was now on him. In 2012, Thanom was trapped by Thai Port fans in their stadium after he decided to award a highly dubious late penalty that relegated the Khlong Toey Army following the 2-1 home defeat to Samut Songkhram. He told the fans he would never referee again – until he got free of the stadium. The next season, in 2013, was his worst. On 4 July he officiated the game between Police United and Buriram, which was won 1-0 by Buriram. This was a result that would come back to haunt him, with near-fatal consequences. In April that year, he was suspended by the AFC for alleged match-fixing and then, on 4 September, he was shot and seriously injured early one morning when leaving his accommodation. A year after this apparent assassination attempt, he was told/persuaded/cajoled to swear an oath at the Temple of the Emerald Buddha promising that he had never taken a bribe or made a mistake, and will never take a bribe or make a mistake.

This was a breathtaking and faintly ridiculous commitment that fooled very few people and only brought his reputation into even more heightened disrepute. Two years later his attacker was given life in prison. So premeditated murder racks up a five-year sentence but out in three, while three shots in a failed assassination attempt gets you a life sentence. Thanom has always vehemently protested his innocence and impartiality. When asked about his conduct by the *Bangkok Post* he replied: 'My decisions were as straight as a ruler.'

So, the next time you want to draw around corners, you know who to ask. In some ways, Thanom was simply a useful idiot for powerful men he would never be able to say no to. His choices were stark and understandable. Do his masters' bidding, or return to a suite at the Bangkok Hilton, one of the world's most notorious prisons. In some ways, it was the Thai FA who should be ashamed as they left him isolated and exposed at a vulnerable time, although you could argue that murdering his boss didn't help his cause either.

Strangely, despite regularly seeing him from the touchline, I didn't expect to be sharing a wedding party a month after my oversized student team photo fail at the Muang Thong Stadium. I was somehow on the guest list of one of the year's biggest social events, a breathtakingly lavish affair. The son of Siam Sports president and SCG Muang Thong United chairman

Ravi Lohtong, Wiluck (or 'Pok'), withstood the gruelling Thai wedding day (rather like an Indian wedding, it is very much a marathon rather than a sprint for the increasingly exhausted couples) before a huge reception at the Impact Arena ballrooms only metres from the stadium. In the previous weeks, the couple had toured all the key European capital cities to capture images of them in front of the iconic buildings that were framed as we entered the huge ballroom teeming with awestruck onlookers. The great and good (and my wife and I) were there from the world of showbusiness, media and sports. Oceans of drink and mountains of food were delivered around the edge of the room, while a gargantuan wedding cake dominated the centre. When I say dominated, I mean three times the height of the bride and groom. As thousands of guests networked furiously, only one referee seemed to have made the guest list. Thanom Borikut appeared to feel right at home in the lavish surroundings, but what was his connection to the event? Whatever the reason, he didn't act like a man who had snuck on to the list as an afterthought and there was no embarrassment shown by those who came to speak to him.

15

Could This Be It?
Interviewing Mr Singha Beer

ON 3 May 2013 I seemed to have made a big breakthrough (again) with a visit to the office of the heir and chief executive officer of the Singha Corporation empire, Chutinant 'Nick' Bhirombhakdi. The progress to get to this point had been slow, almost glacial. Three years earlier I had started at the bottom of the Singha Corporation food chain by inviting one of their staff to the Women Wear Red evening hosted by my wife in our Harrow VIP box at the Thunderdome. Then, through my job at Harrow and building connections in Thai football, I was able to reach one layer of the corporate ladder higher every few months until, remarkably, I found myself in the office of the heir to the Singha fortune. Knowing how these things work in Thai football, I also knew (but of course could never say) that Bangkok Glass president and fellow family member Pawin Bhirombhakdi had put a good family word in for me to get this meeting over the line.

Yet again I was grateful to my *L'Équipe* photographer friend Pascal's very reasonable rates of zero as he joined me in Nick's palatial offices. I had been through the questions I wanted to ask, but also the sponsorship I was seeking, to convert this VSO-style income to something that at least gave a little return on my time investment. Waiting outside, there was an intimidating row of workers seated at desks outside Nick's office all highly busy and deep in thought. If I could get half an hour, I would try to earn their boss's trust before asking for the money shot of some recognition and remuneration. When we were called in, every eventuality had been pre-planned. If he was whisked off rapidly soon after we started, we would make sure we took photos early so at least we would have that to prove the meeting happened. I had printed out copies of the sponsorship requests so I could pass them to one of his underlings if everything stopped before we had a chance to develop a rapport. I needn't have worried.

We ended up spending almost an hour with Nick. He was gracious, friendly and, most surprisingly, not busy. I remember being stunned that his desk phone didn't ring once and he gave the impression of a man who seemed to enjoy our company so we could be part of it for as long as we wanted to. After the interview questions finished and the three of us sat together talking amiably, Nick seemed genuinely interested in what I was trying to do (his English was flawless after his international education). This had started at the Hotchkiss School – a coeducational prep school in Lakeville, Connecticut. After Hotchkiss, Nick went on to Boston University, Then, unusually for a Thai child educating abroad, instead of coming home to help run the family business, he joined the European American Bank in New York City.

Nick was, like AIA's Ron van Oijen, a highly successful and powerful person whose true passion was sport. Used to careerist underlings looking for favour and advancement, both men seemed comfortable in the company of fellow sports fans, even if his speciality was different to ours. I could see this with Ron when we played for his AIA charity team together on the Muang Thong pitch (where I broke Thai protocol by chipping the powerful but diminutive keeper twice to seal a win and social ignominy). Nick's passion was martial arts, but I picked up immediately that what bonded us together were the elements that all sports engender.

Talking to the in-house Hotchkiss magazine in September 2016, Nick highlighted the way his favourite sport specifically (he was a third-degree black belt in Shotokan Karate) and sport in general would make certain demands on us in return for advancement: 'Karate teaches you to resist instant gratification and to focus on long-term and meaningful goals.'

The three of us recognised similar values and passion. The hour flew by and we left with the feeling that Nick would rather spend his time talking in detail about sport than doing his day job, which was fine by us. Of course, the sponsorship came to nought, rather like the agreement Ron signed off that was sabotaged by bean-counting underlings. But we had felt a kinship with a fellow sports fan who just happened to be managing a billion-dollar industry and, as with Ron, I got the strong sense that he would rather be doing our job than his, despite my conspicuous lack of funds.

16

Interviewing the King of Buriram

THAI CULTURE and language centre around a strong sense of deference and respect. Even a strongly worded statement is expected to be ended by not one but two 'politeness particles'. The first is 'nah', and the second is 'kah' for female speakers and 'kap' for males, which is sometimes replaced with 'krap' for added politeness. This obsession with avoiding confrontation showed itself in what I always called a 'death by yesses'. Every suggestion was greeted by affirmation to avoid the risk of upsetting me, but the agreement had no basis in action or planning. The 'yes' was simply to tick a box that kept the foreigner happy, which I assumed meant the project was being prepared for me to complete. Not only (like the VIP box stadium visit by the Harrow parents) was nothing being put in motion, but the project had often been instantly forgotten as soon as the 'yes/chai nah kap' was mouthed. Coupled with the *greng jai* conventions, this consistently tied me up in knots and had me rolling out the jaundiced phrase to my wife that 'the early bird gets shat on from a great height'.

Confused? Get in the queue. Another challenge to a westerner trying to bend their mind around this tonal, Sanskrit-inflected and hierarchical language is that, even though sentences seem to be a soft shoed dance of dereference, the word 'please' is rarely used and the kind of constructs we often use like 'would you mind if' are jettisoned in favour of the much-blunter sounding 'I want' or 'I need'. But one thing is certain, words, supported by *wais* that subtly signify the hierarchical relationship between speaker and listener by the height of the clasped hands (the higher up the fingers, the further up the respect dial you are), blend a heady mixture of blunt, grammar-free sentences with complex layers of social nuance. But then there is Newin Chidchop. Appropriately as a man from the northeast, Newin reminded me of a bluff Yorkshireman. He only deals in hard nos or hard yesses. This was probably a challenge in his previous storied political career. Newin was always seen as a Marmite figure, but I liked him from the start despite (or maybe because of) some of the stories that surrounded him. If there was a Thai sentence for 'I know what I like and I like what I know' then he was the man to say it (and very few people would be wise to argue).

I was standing on the side of a Bangkok road with Pascal, waiting for Buriram's team manager Tadthep Pitakpulsin, who had kindly volunteered to drive us the arduous 312km journey up north. I'd briefly met Tadthep at matches before and he was an excellent English speaker with a gentle and disarming personality. All through the journey, he was friendly and very open about some of the bizarre things happening behind the scenes with the AFC. Looking back on it now, this journey was part job interview, part trust audit. If we didn't pass, there would be no club access and, more importantly, no interview with Newin.

The journey passed affably with the three of us swapping stories of our strange experiences in Thai football. Several hours later, Tadthep delivered us to our hotel and that's where things started to become off-kilter and slightly surreal. I felt like Truman Burbank in the film *The Truman Show* and it was something I was to experience when working for Buriram's great rival at the time, Bangkok's Muang Thong United in 2010. After years of dominance from the Kirins (Muang Thong's nickname), Buriram were starting to chip away at the annual procession of titles and there was no love lost between the clubs. I travelled up to Buriram with the team and the first odd thing I noticed was how we were forbidden from staying in Buriram itself. Everything seemed slightly hyper-normal in that *Truman Show* way as we seemed to all be walking on eggshells but trying to pretend this was normal. Newin had been a powerful 'kingmaker' in Thai politics who could swap sides faster than Jermaine Pennant (who would trial at Muang Thong in 2016 before ending up at Singapore's Tampines Rovers). Then I realised I had forgotten my toothbrush. I strolled breezily through the lobby where club coaches and periphery staff always seem to camp out and casually told the management team I was heading off to the nearest 7-11. But, as soon as I stepped outside the hotel doors, I was joined on the trip by an armed guard. When I got to the shop, I could hardly pick the brush up for shaking. Despite winning the Thai Premier League that year, this was one of Muang Thong's three defeats all season and the 1-0 loss seemed the safest way to get out of there without further anxiety.

For this visit to Buriram with Pascal, I went to the reception to check in and that's where the astonishing three-day experience started to unveil itself. We presented our passports, ready to explain why we were there. At the time, Buriram was a dusty and far-off province rarely explored by tourists. Now, Newin's 32,600-capacity Chang Arena King Power clone, with its car-racing track and four-star Amari Hotel is a different world from that five-hour car journey to a tired provincial hotel. He even built a nearby airport to comply with AFC regulations about proximity to international connections, as you do. But in 2013, we were a curiosity that we felt needed an explanation. There was no need. Everyone seemed to already know exactly who we were and why we were there. The staff seemed nervous, almost fearful. Certainly not the kind of impression I usually make at a Premier Inn. The reception area was a standard two-star dispiriting Thai hotel but behind it was a brand-new, conspicuous and outsized TV: something that would chill me 24 hours later. For now, Pascal and I unpacked before meeting back in a coffee shop near the reception, where I went through the questions I would put to Newin. After a pleasant hour, we were ready for Tadthep to pick us up. At the time, it was tricky getting around the area with precious few taxis and even fewer English speakers (to my shame, my Thai never really rose above the tonal-deaf beginner, despite our 16-year stay in the kingdom) so we were grateful for a lift in the brain-melting heat this province specialised in. It was a little surprising that Tadthep, the team manager, had been assigned as our taxi driver a day before a vital last-16 AFC Champions League game against Uzbekistan Super League's Bunyodkor. How many owners of a club that size would make their right-hand man available to a low-to-no-profile football writer and his photographer?

I remember, as we passed groups of chatting lobby guests, their volume seemed to drop down to mute. I was too focused on running through the questions in my head for the Big Boss to really take this in, but it was an increasingly bizarre scenario. A few minutes later we arrived at the practice pitch where we had agreed to meet Newin and this was when I saw his inner Yorkshireman unleashed. On reflection, it was probably an intimidation audit for me but, after working with Muang Thong coach René Desaeyere, I was used to dealing with alpha males. Newin wanted me to interview him on the pitch. Two suited and lanyard-heavy AFC goons decided this would contravene some arcane bylaw and came over to shush us away. Big mistake. It reminded me of a scene in our favourite film *In Bruges* where the tour operator aggressively explains to Harry Waters (chillingly played by Ralph Fiennes) that the Belfry of Bruges is closed. It didn't end well.

Newin went full Geoff Boycott on them and they soon disappeared like salted snails. So, intimidation audit complete, I was next up as the wounded AFC careerists glowered from a safe distance. No pressure there then. The interview went smoothly. Newin professed to have very little English and would often defer to Tadthep for answers, but I got the feeling he could express himself in English just fine. He was keeping me on the back foot (as if he needed to try) in a way I often saw in contract negotiations with English-speaking coaches. Starting in English, when it came to the key details, a swift switch to the most colloquial of Thai would help derail any momentum the foreigner may have been experiencing.

After the interview, we went on to the stadium for some background photos and popped in to say hi to Buriram's English coach Scott Cooper. We stayed for a few minutes of the typically banal AFC pre-match press conference before making our way back to the hotel so Pascal could select his key photos and I could write up the interview. When I greeted the receptionist to request my room key he was keen to guide my gaze to the outsized TV screen. On it was footage of me as I greeted and interviewed Newin and footage of my day. I hadn't seen or noticed the cameraman following me.

Message received. I walked up the stairs to my room on legs of barely set jelly.

The next day was less surreal, but no less enjoyable. Arriving at the stadium in the early afternoon, we took shelter from the relentless heat in the stadium coffee shop. Weirdly, the 7-11 building next to it was completely wrapped in industrial paper and none of their own branded products were on sale as they weren't AFC sponsors. Walking around the impressive stadium in the late afternoon I was surprised to be invited in by Scott for an interview in his office. If he was nervous, it certainly didn't show. Everything, from pitchside passes to stadium access was organised with seamless efficiency (something I wasn't used to when dealing with the Thai FA), and Scott's team went on to give a tactical masterclass in their 2-1 victory. So shocked were the Bunyodkor coaches that they sent their whole bench to warm up a quarter of an hour into the game: something I've rarely seen before or since. After chatting late into the evening with Scott and his family in the bowels of the stadium, the club kindly let me jump in the spaceship-like team bus that, inside a standard coach exterior, had an airtight inner section that was over-oxygenated to help injury recovery. Tired but hyper-awake at 3am back on the outskirts of Bangkok, this weird jumble of emotions seemed entirely fitting for a bonkers, life-affirming 72 hours. You just couldn't make it up.

16

AFC Champions League (Dis)qualification

THIS IS a good time to try and explain a social contract it took me years to understand, but is central to the way many Thais interact. Underpinning this implicit understanding of social norms is the approach known as *greng jai*. Roughly translated, it means 'spirit fear' but is more like the English phrase of 'I'm afraid that'. From there, similarities to how we socially interact in the west are left behind. It is the action of not telling someone something that may harm or anger them. Simply put, western culture would label this lying. But in Thai culture, this is an act of ultimate respect. Like most interactions in Thailand, it is based on hierarchy. If there is a problem that needs fixing with someone above you, then it is unlikely to be brought up, even if it has highly negative consequences.

So there I was bent double over the team-bus barrier staring into the football abyss. An FA Cup semi-final defeat to Chonburi had consigned Suphanburi to miss out on a season in which they had a realistic chance of reaching the final. All the stars had aligned that year to knock out SCG Muang Thong United and the kingdom's strongest club, Buriram United. Since the competition was relaunched in 2008, apart from its first season back, all semi-finals had included one or both of the clubs, so a narrow defeat to the Sharks with the inconsistent and mid-table Bangkok Glass waiting in the final was a jagged pill to swallow.

From the other side of the barrier, one of my colleagues looked surprised and embarrassed by my dejection. 'Jai yen yen. Next year we win!' *Jai yen yen* roughly translates to 'very cold heart'; a surprising phrase for such generally warm-hearted people. But it wasn't only my colleagues who responded in this classically Thai fashion. As I sat on the team bus waiting to go, the Chonburi and Suphanburi staff mingled happily (which was good to see) but the joy seemed evenly spread between both clubs. If I hadn't been to the match, deciphering which team was one match from an AFC adventure and whose season essentially had just ended would have been a challenge.

As a foreigner, it's a strange call to make. Being in the middle of this scene, I started to feel oddly selfish for being so disappointed. It seemed like my response was inappropriate and too negative, wrong-footing me and showing just how disparately different hemispheres approach the same love of football. Part of the tranquillity is to prevent losing face. Our president left the stadium as soon as the game had finished, so gusts of grief like professional mourners at Kim Jong-il's funeral would have drawn too much attention to our collective failure.

From a western point of view, we have to show how much losing hurts to ensure we do it as little as possible (unless we support Aston Villa). The Thai approach to failure is often denial (previous FAT head Worawi Makudi's 'shock' at Thailand's rank of 158 being a laughable example) and it stunts the ability of the Thai game to improve. From the five stages of grief, Thai football only signs up to the first, Crisis, and the third, Upheaval. They ignore stage two, Unity, rarely demonstrate an appetite for stage four, Resolution, and only reluctantly address the final stage of Renewal if they are forced to by an outside agency. In Sir Chris Hoy's excellent BBC documentary, *How To Win Gold*, he inadvertently highlighted how Thai football is losing half the battle, 'Champions are made by endless hard work and determination, by victory and defeat.'

I found this out to my cost when working for a provincial football club in 2015. Struggling under the incendiary regime of a vampiric-looking Bulgarian coach (more of him later), he was finally dispensed with in December the previous year and replaced with the classy and tactically astute Brazilian Sérgio Farias who, uniquely for a club with a carousel of coaches, would return a year later after resigning on 13 August of the 2015 season. Sérgio had a storied pedigree. Having won the K League in 2007 and the AFC Champions League in 2009 with Pohang Steelers, he'd also been Brazil's under-17 coach and was a man of outstanding tactical ability. How on earth we got him I will never know but I was privileged to share a few months with the man. When he left, the club had just surprisingly lost at home to a single goal by a team who would eventually finish the season in 14th place, but the club were still in a strong position and the decision was a big surprise when we could see the training-ground progress being made every week. He had assembled a strong core of foreign players from Brazil, South Korea, Spain and Indonesia. The impressive collection included the defensive Brazilian colossus Márcio Rozário whose spells at Botafogo and Fluminense showed his true level, but off-field activities (especially with presidents' daughters) had made him a footballing nomad, with 18 clubs at the last count. He was a phenomenal signing for a Thai team and it suited him to be relatively out of the limelight.

Two other key foreign players were the Rolls-Royce midfielder Carmelo González who had surprisingly signed from Thai heavyweights Buriram United after over a century of games with Spanish club Las Palmas and a dozen caps for Spain's under-21s. Oddly, four years later when we were living in the beautiful Spanish city, we bumped into him again while he was picking up his daughter from the kindergarten my wife was working at. Completing the foreign quota (Thai clubs could sign three players from anywhere, one more from within the AFC (Asian Football Confederation) and three from ASEAN at the time) was the Dutch/

Indonesian Sergio van Dijk. This is a rule that, after half a decade, was revised in 2022. Now there are five global places, one AFC slot and unlimited ASEAN players in the squad. Rather like the five subs rule, this will only serve to further strengthen the hands of clubs that can summon vast resources. Leading the line like an old-school centre-forward, the affable and highly player would play 40 times for the club that year before surprisingly (to him as much as to the fans) being released. His 14 goals that season were vital to the club's success but he was also supported by high-quality Thai players like the Swiss/Thai midfielder Charyl Chappuis and a host of other Thai internationals.

Despite a point in the first game, I could see that we had the squad, coach and style of play to do something special. A 2-2 draw against Buriram United on 7 March was a useful yardstick where, despite being two goals down, Van Dijk equalised with two minutes to go. After three wins in a row, the next defeat would come away to Chiang Rai United. If you ever go to the northern city, I highly recommend a matchday there. The stadium is partly modelled on Villa Park (the second one in Thai football; the other is one of the stands at Singha Corporation-owned BG Pathum United). It's also only a five-minute walk from the airport and has a really old-school English football stadium feel, but with warmer weather and cheaper beer. Behind the main stand, the northern hills shield the sunsets that begin as games start, providing an incredibly beer-infused, iridescent backdrop to games.

Working as a 'photographer' (an unskilled doughnut with a camera would be a better title), I once made one too many calls to the pre-match bar. With the home team winning and choosing to waste every remaining second, I woozily found myself staggering on to the pitch to remonstrate with the prone player in front of 15,000 shocked fans. Luckily for me, security didn't know how to handle a drunk 6ft foreigner so decided discretion was the better form of valour and left me to slowly realise my mistake.

Despite that defeat to Chiang Rai, the club were in second place in the league and even four draws in a row after that and a fall to sixth couldn't dampen the mood that this was a special group of players ably orchestrated by a knowledgeable coach. The next five games gave us four wins and a draw to move back up to fourth, but four 1-0 defeats on the bounce seemed to have derailed our season, especially the final one in the sequence which resulted in Farias's resignation. This was so harsh on him. He had set the tone and embedded the tactics but would not be part of the successes to come. That honour was given to journeyman Thai Worrawoot Srimaka in his second of three short spells with the club. The new coach bounce was rewarded by three wins and a draw but the season seemed to be fizzling out when two consecutive defeats left them in a mediocre seventh place in this 18-team league.

Then, somehow, the last three months of the season caught fire. Sergio van Dijk scored five times in an undefeated eight-match sequence and, by the time we played Army United on 9 December, we knew that a win for us and defeats for rivals Chonburi and Bangkok United would secure an unlikely AFC Champions League spot for next season after starting the day in fifth place and with both our rivals playing at home against clubs in danger of relegation. We strolled to a 3-0 win and, on the final whistle, news started to filter through that Chonburi had lost 1-0 to the intriguingly named Osotspa (pharmaceuticals) M-150 (rancid caffeine syrup) Samut Prakan and Bangkok United could only draw with doomed TOT who went down rock bottom after three wins from 34 attempts. So both our rivals had failed to capitalise, against a team whose win secured their league survival and one who had nothing to play for after an abysmal season but still managed to stir themselves enough to force a 1-1 draw stunningly after being behind with only half an hour of their season left. Now we were in the qualifiers for Asia's biggest tournament. Rubbing shoulders with high-profile teams from across the region would be our chance to cement a place at the top table. We all ran on to the Army United pitch to celebrate with the players and salute our thousands of travelling fans. This was going to be some adventure. The final game of the season was an after the Lord Mayor's Show event when a 2-2 draw with Chonburi's victors led to more celebrations and dreams of Asian travel.

It had been a hectic last few weeks for us all, so I took a break with my wife in the Thai resort of Hua Hin, treating ourselves to a stay in the luxurious

Centara Grand Beach Resort. I was floating on air, running through how we would spread the reach of English media for Thai football across the region and heighten the profile of Suphanburi FC. One morning we decided to have breakfast on the terrace overlooking the sea, thinking of the relaxing day ahead. Then I had a phone call from the club's general manager that was short, to the point and chilling. 'Do you have the phone number for the AFC?' Instantly I knew something was wrong. After plenty of hesitation, he eventually told me how the club had not processed the required paperwork and that our place in the 2016 competition was in doubt. As soon as I put the phone down, I called AFC headquarters in Kuala Lumpur (you can imagine how delighted my wife was to have yet another day hijacked by football). After a short, professional response from the man on the other end, it became clear that our expulsion for lack of paperwork and stadium facilities (especially a lack of seating and the need for additional roofing on one of the stands) was already under way. You could argue that, with eight games to go sitting in seventh place, complying with AFC Champions League regulations may have seemed arrogant, but the club could have sourced other stadiums in Bangkok that complied and used them for Champions League games. Instead, until it was too late, nothing was done and this was partly due to *greng jai*. Complaining upwards is a big no-no, so club officials sat on any information that needed acting on, especially as there was an implied criticism of the club's current facilities. Something else

I learned about face-saving was that, returning for the next season, the subject was never referred to. It was as if it had never happened and bringing it up would have been the first step towards the exit door for anyone who dared to do so.

This dispiriting feeling of missed opportunities was sharpened on 21 January 2020. After winning the previous season's FA Cup, Bangkok's Port FC also qualified for the AFC Champions League and had a non-compliant stadium. But, rather than forfeit the home advantage to another ground in the kingdom (I still can't understand how this didn't happen with my club half a decade earlier), the club did an overnight ground development to comply with regulations. Slapdash seats were hastily installed and coats of paint applied to the crumbling surfaces ready to take on Ceres-Negros (renamed United City for the tournament to avoid giving their bus company sponsors any undue profile) from the Philippines in a game the Thais were confident of winning. The Port Lions ended up surrendering tamely to a single-goal defeat when the chance to visit Japan and test themselves against FC Tokyo was waiting for the winners. I never shook off the feeling that five years earlier we were better equipped for the next stages compared to our replacements Chonburi, who would be destroyed 9-0 by Tokyo in February 2016 in a final qualification match after squeezing past Myanmar's Yangon United after extra time in the first qualification round. Maybe it was better that Port didn't get to play in Japan after all.

Whenever a new coach came to Thailand from the west I tried to warn them about invading their players' personal space or shouting at them to make an example. I hoped (and failed) to give them insight into *greng jai* and the idea that, by making a player lose face, there would be a consequence that happened at any point in the future. The conflict will have been forgotten by the westerner, but it was a time bomb buried deep in the consciousness of the Thai player that may not go off for years, but explode it certainly would. Not in a spectacular outpouring of violence that you might see elsewhere, but a subtle and equally destructive missed pass or scuffed penalty that would result in disappointment for the player and a sacking for the foreign coach. Losing face is a concept familiar to most Asian countries and is founded on consideration and respect for others, but *greng jai* is a much more complex dance that both sides need to understand or one of them will stumble and tumble into social minefields.

This was something I really struggled with once I was part of the Thai football world. Let me give you an example. One day I had a call from the boss of a club I was working with that said he wanted to meet me. So I battled through the traffic and, two hours later, arrived at the club's main headquarters. Giving myself a margin of safety, I arrived early and had a coffee across the road before arriving ten minutes before the appointment which I was told was important. An hour later I sat there steaming with anger and frustration. Half an hour on, I started to storm out, which was when one of the support staff chased me down and pleaded with me to stay. Even though I had arrived as planned and the director hadn't bothered to show up, it was my responsibility to apologise for the meeting's failure. This would have ensured that both sides retained face and no friction was caused. Over the years, as I let go and (slightly) succumbed to it, I realised there was a deeper layer to explore for those that accepted it. If I had apologised (I didn't by the way) then my no-show colleague would have implicitly been in my debt. Even though we would never mention it, there would be a time when he repaid me. It could happen tomorrow or in ten years, but this would always be honoured. As it was, by not playing the game, I was later banned from the club by him for three months because one of my colleagues lied about not being at work and I hadn't shared that with the club. I now had a taste of reverse *greng jai*.

Another unusual aspect of how the uber-powerful rulers of Thai business and politics behave is that, for the mighty beasts with unlimited power, you can spot them because they are the ones who constantly downgrade their influence. I was at a kit launch for Muang Thong United in 2005 at my local shopping mall on a road called Chaeng Watthana. After the event, we crossed over the footbridge to share a meal with some of the club's sponsors in a tower block called Software Park. During the meal, a man with excellent English started chatting to me and seemed genuinely interested in what I was trying to do in Thai football.

As someone who worked in the building, he told me he enjoyed having a local football club on his doorstep and was pleased that his company were supporting the club. It was only after we had all dispersed ready to go back to the stadium that someone told me the man not only worked there but owned the whole building. It also turned out that what I thought were standard Thai noodle dishes had been cooked using Italian oil. When stocks were getting low, he chartered a plane to get a few more bottles direct from the Italian source. For him to have revealed this to me would have been bad form. If it wasn't for my vice-president Pok telling me, I would never have known.

18

Gatecrashing Manchester United's Pity Party

BACK IN July 2013, we were outside Bangkok's swanky Four Seasons Hotel. Bryan Robson was returning to the kingdom for one of the first times since his two-year tenure as Thai national coach between 2009 and 2011, after taking over from fellow Englishman Peter Reid. Now in his role as Manchester United's global ambassador, little did I know then that two years later we would both be sharing an afternoon among the United squad, as football groupies and hangers-on swarmed around us. We'd kept in touch over the interim and he'd agreed to let me interview him for a football website I was working on called Thai League Football.

This was my second attempt. A few days earlier we had agreed to do it at the elegant Shangrila Hotel on Bangkok's riverside. I waited with my hideously expensive coffee (everything was hideously expensive with me pulling in precisely zero from this work). I waited, and waited, and waited. Eventually, with cold coffee in hand, I realised that Bryan was not turning up. So I put this down as one more expense to add to my wife's unintended financial sponsorship. Bryan messaged me to apologise and invited me to interview him again later at the Four Seasons when Manchester United would be making what was their fifth visit to the kingdom, albeit their first in 12 years.

This time I went all in. I invited Buriram's coach Scott Cooper and my long-suffering and unpaid photographer friend Pascal. When the three of us arrived at the hotel, it was bedlam. I hadn't considered how we could prove we were there to meet Robbo as security was bound to be inundated with lunatics telling them they knew Wayne Rooney or Rio Ferdinand. Luckily the security guards recognised Scott and led us into a lobby rammed with serious Red Devils fanatics who travelled the world in obsessive pursuit of the club. This was the hardcore inner circle with many of them clutching historic memorabilia for one more signature as an empty replacement for conversation. They were a tight unit of globetrotters and resented us arrivistes breaking into their inner sanctum. We sat down and surveyed the scene, surrounded by United players looking morose and bored to the bone. So this was it. Either Bryan would show up or we would have to reverse traverse through the hordes of hangers-on pretending that we had only popped in to sample their superior coffee.

To add to the tension, we had been shown to an alpha table furthest away from the access-free fans, outside and nearest to the players. I remember sheepishly looking up from my coffee to see Rio Ferdinand glaring down at me in a 'you don't belong here' challenge. But then, something magical happened. The frantic foyer quietened for a moment and, like some kind of Hollywood cliche, Bryan glided down the marble staircase and called across, telling me, 'Hi, Matt, sorry I'm a bit late.' With that, everything was changed and rearranged. Like actors taking up their new marks in a movie, the hardcore fans now wanted favours from us with direct access to club legends. Players melted back into the shadows and the five of us (Bryan's assistant and interpreter Wasapol Kaewpaluk had joined us) spent an hour that felt like sitting on a calm iceberg in a frothing sea of madness. Bryan was genuinely interested in Scott's progress at Buriram and seemed relieved to be with someone he had known and trusted after he visited Harrow. Despite the financial suicide that a foreigner trying to make a living commits to, I glided out of that hotel after an hour that had taken two years to construct feeling as if I had just cashed in a million-pound cheque.

For Manchester United, that tour was to be the beginning of the end for David Moyes, something that was pretty obvious when we witnessed his scratchy-at-best time with the players. They even managed to lose the cash drop game against an over-optimistically named Thai All-Stars the next day. But none of that mattered to me. I now had a bona fide star interview to open doors and spread the word about Thai football in

English across Asia. Of course, none of that happened, but it was a wonderful moment to crouch inside and dream.

19

Tesco Lotus Tournaments.
Every Little Helps

IN JUNE 2011, as one of the perks of doing all the hard yards to set up and run a football team (and having a marketing budget to siphon into new kits and tournament fees), I got to share the pitch with some ageing legends as self-appointed captain. I even had the privilege of missing a penalty in the final against these stars which, Professor Brian Cox may confirm, is still travelling in space to this day.

Starting early on a Saturday morning, everyone aimed to stagger through a series of rounds in the increasingly sapping heat and line up against Ian Rush, Lee Sharpe and Steve McMahon among a collection of regional sports reporters and the odd local player drafted in to do the legwork. This was the BCCT (British Chamber of Commerce Thailand) Tesco Lotus Bangkok Masters Seven-a-Side Football Tournament and was, for a few short years, the highlight of pub-level players and aspiring athletes across the kingdom. The two-day event at Thailand's first International School, Bangkok Patana, was a war of attrition with 37 teams fighting off the intense heat, father time and the massive temptation after the Saturday games to rehydrate in Bangkok's many distracting watering holes. We already had an advantage over teams coming from the UK, Netherlands, Canada, Australia, China, Japan, Hong Kong, Malaysia, Singapore, Brunei and Vietnam that this was not a once-in-a-lifetime opportunity to explore what Bangkok nightlife had to offer but for us as 'locals' was a pleasure that could be deferred for another time. The touring parties filled their football boots after the Saturday games and arrived on Sunday looking like salted snails and not fit for footballing purposes. The teams we knew would pose the biggest risks were the locals and those from Phuket and Pattaya that, if they could resist Bangkok's pleasures for one night, would come into the Sunday games raring to go.

We managed to navigate the early rounds, relying on fast starts with our young Thai legs and a mass defence. It also helped that the huge pitches and continual timers meant that one of my row Z clearances would waste valuable seconds as already fatigued opponents would need to trot across several other pitches to retrieve the ball. My cunning two-pronged plan was to bring along some of our Thai school cooks who could run all day and put the 6ft 4in Chris 'Rocky' Rock in the scaled-down goals to intimidatingly fill the space. He was also an excellent keeper so, using waves of speed and Thai skill in the early rounds, we managed to make it to the final against the stars. This was where I put my Alamo defence in place, something that annoyed the heck out of Steve McMahon who could regularly be heard shouting, 'You can come out of your own fucking half, you know.'

Despite our Alamo efforts, they took the lead through Lee Sharpe, forcing us to stick or twist. I decided we would continue to keep it tight and hope, as they tired, we would get a chance to equalise and take the game to penalties. Ian Rush was struggling in the heat, but McMahon and Sharpe had clearly continued to train after their career ended and were a constant threat. So, as we came to the last few seconds of the game I threw all the Thai players on and they did it. A great run down the right, a cross and then a tidy finish meant that we had taken the stars to penalties with Big Rocky dominating the goal. Unfortunately, one of the Thai lads missed his kick which meant that, after Rush and Sharpe slotted past Rocky (some skills don't dissipate with age), I needed to score if we were to keep our chances alive. I calmly strode up to the ball and decided to give it the full Frank Lampard senior (look it up, kids). Unfortunately, with great power came no responsibility and my shot ballooned over the bar with me standing watching it sail over the changing-room roof.

The day finished with an enjoyable evening at a local hotel, The Landmark, and I am sure the organisers were relieved that it was photos of the winning stars in the next day's *Bangkok Post* rather than us. That's exactly what I was thinking when I ran up to take my kick.

20

The Thai Tiger King

THERE TENDS to be three different levels of Thai football club owners: gold, silver and bronze. In the bronze category, you've got the slicked-back Brylcreem hair, sunglasses indoors-wearing, perpetually black-suited brigade. They surround themselves with an entourage of barely concealed weapon-toting bodyguards. In the silver category comes those who only retain one or two bodyguards with the black inky eyes that have seen things you don't even want to read about. Some will be ex-special forces or retired Muay Thai champions. Some of them don't even bother tooling up. If you say or do the wrong thing, you'll probably wish you'd been shot by the time they finish with you. The gold-standard powerbrokers are small in number but vast in power. They dispense with any security because the consequences for you, your family, friends or milkman of you doing anything to challenge them are too dire to even contemplate. This leads me nicely to a trip up north to Chiang Mai.

René had spent almost exactly one year at Muang Thong United in his first spell, which started in that pre-season on 11 January and would end with his sacking during pre-season on 7 January the following year. In the meantime, his team had won the Thai Premier League, been runners-up in the FA Cup, got to the play-offs of the AFC Champions League and reached the semi-finals of the second-tier AFC Cup. René's players were just squeezed out in the semi-finals 2-1 by the eventual winners from Syria, Al-Ittihad, despite the Thais winning the first leg 1-0. Oh, and of course, as I mentioned earlier, René was voted Coach of the Year for Thai football.

So, here René and I were just a few weeks after the sacking, talking to a club freshly out of the regional leagues and joining the second level with huge ambitions of shaking up Thai football. We decided to fly up to the president's province to keep René's name being talked about, as a combination of his big personality and a fear of annoying Siam Sport kept other suitors at arm's length. So up to Chiang Mai we went.

All started as planned. We arrived at the cavernous Seven Hundred Year Anniversary Stadium, which we soon realised was rarely even a quarter full, with a plan to discuss what the actual details of any offer would be before deciding if we would accept or reject it. Unfortunately, their president had other ideas. Arriving in the club offices at the agreed time we were left to sit there and stew for a fraught two hours where René was all for walking straight out and jumping back on the next plane. The poor staff must have sensed this and were petrified of telling their boss that we had been allowed to leave. In a meal we shared with him later, he ticked all the 'wrong 'un' boxes, including working 'in construction': somewhere I assume many of his competitors found themselves. Having hung us out to dry for long enough, the president finally decided to arrive. He met us briefly and perfunctorily, which was odd as, at the Amari Airport Bangkok a few days later to announce René's eventual signing, the charm taps had been opened to full. Without any warning, he took us out to the waiting players and announced that René was now their new coach. I could see this spinning out of control quickly. He even instructed René to train them then and there. This was going to be a long day. Not surprisingly, René refused, and the stage was set for a battle of wills. I mentally flicked through my life insurance to confirm that a mysterious but fatal gardening accident in Thailand was covered. The temperature wasn't lowered by the fact that the president had also invited members of the press to commemorate this important event. After plenty of toing and froing, in a kind of Mexican standoff, it was finally agreed to adjourn to the president's palatial house for further negotiations. We thought this would buy us breathing space and some moment of clarity. How wrong we were.

As you'll see from the photograph taken by my friend Pascal in the picture section (unpaid as ever), this was no ordinary contract negotiation. His first gambit was to dive into the tiger's cage in his extensive driveway (yes, it is illegal to keep tigers as pets in Thailand). Being toyed with by a fully grown tiger was the president with one of his bodyguards having drawn the short straw of jumping into the cage to make sure his boss didn't become the tiger's next afternoon snack. On reflection, the not too subtle statement being made to us was that, in this scenario, there is a tiger and its prey. And I'm not the prey. With this alpha-male posturing complete, we made our way into his house with the growing feeling that we were getting entangled in something it would be impossible to break free from. Entering his house, the first thing I noticed was how it was casually littered with priceless antiques. Ming vases, Japanese full suits of ceremonial armour and fine art were propped up wherever there was space, like so many pairs of unwanted socks.

He was not a man used to negotiating, making the process as pleasant as pulling teeth without an anaesthetic. I got the feeling the only time he heard the word 'no' was when something much more painful than a coaching contract was being foisted on someone. After hours of intransigence, I decided to excuse myself and wander back out to the courtyard for some air. As I walked out of the room, on my left-hand side a dozing guard was startled by my movement. Instinctively, he reached into his jacket to remove his gun. If there weren't red flags before, we now had an idea of what we were getting into. On reflection, foolishly, we decided to agree on a deal. The terms weren't what we had hoped for, but there seemed huge potential in the club and, with a city of over 100,000 people, there also seemed to be vast potential for club growth coupled with the plans, we were told, to develop the stadium, training ground (then on the top of a hill with no netting, so stray balls would travel hundreds of metres away before being retrieved) and create a partnership with the local international school that had excellent facilities.

But what we would soon come to realise was how the president's views of a coach and ours were completely set at odds. Our understanding was that René would need some form of autonomy and say in recruitment. The president felt that he now had another employee just like the workers in his businesses that he needed to tell exactly what to do. That would be borne out in later weeks when, the night before each game, a piece of paper would be slipped under René's bizarre club apartment door showing the team the president had chosen and he expected to see trotting out the next day. With walls covered with purple carpet and full suits of armour dotted around the oversized beds in this dark wood play pad, it was clear what its former use had been in downtown Chiang Rai. The president's team selection criteria were far more profound than ability or a week's good training. For him, players should be picked on character, even if they were currently injured or suspended. But for now, all was smiles and handshakes.

We went down to Bangkok with just one more worrying event. On landing at Bangkok's Don Muang

Airport, a fruit bowl was passed around. But, instead of complimentary fruit, it was piled high with handguns. René was asked which one was his and, when he told them none of them were, he was looked at like a New York cop surveying a Cornish village police station. This was, of course, before we went through security.

The press conference to announce René's arrival was in the Amari Airport Hotel just over a footbridge from the landing bay, the same one we used to go to before every home game for the Muang Thong United players to have breakfast and review tactics before taking a nap in reconfigured conference rooms. René was unveiled as part of a brave new plan for the club and the province. They had captured Thai football's reigning Coach of the Year and were now prepared to crash the top-tier party before dominating the game for years to come. Just the type of nonsense you'd expect to hear. By the end of that season, rather than being top-flight disruptors, they had crashed back down into the regional leagues and René had long since left (taking advantage of the confusion caused by flooding to pack his car full of his belongings and disappear into the night). This was a club determined to shoot itself in the foot and keep firing wildly.

Speaking of which, at one of the home games I flew up to watch, the president (after what he thought was an unfair defeat through poor refereeing) snatched the mic from the PA and asked if anyone in the crowd was armed. If they were, he said, they had a duty to track the official down and make use of their weapon. Madness.

Circled by his staff, they knew he was inviting mayhem, but they were petrified of him and in his pay, so he was allowed to vent and vent until he was spent. René was in the press conference at the time. That was an interesting bar-room conversation later that evening. Perhaps it didn't bode well that the team photo for that season didn't include René. Instead, a photo of him was cut and pasted into the top right-hand corner: something easy to remove if necessary.

Four months after our strange adventure up north, Muang Thong would make one of their highest-profile signings. René had been replaced by Brazilian coach Carlos Roberto, a man with over 400 appearances for Botafogo and a coaching career that had already spanned nearly three decades. He had recently completed a short stint at fellow Thai club Bangkok Glass and, chatting to him as he trained his players at Harrow, I was amazed at his frankness about how he was tired of football and just couldn't motivate himself the way he used to. This was not going to end well and on 28 February 2011, only two months after signing, he was gone. His replacement was a completely different beast. Henrique Calisto had just finished three years coaching the Vietnam national team and was fiercely motivated. He had a stare that could melt asphalt and his training sessions were intense and productive. I could see him having a similar effect as René on the team, forcing them to be more professional on and off the pitch.

Unfortunately for the disciplinarian Calisto, four months into his tenure, Muang Thong decided to go big on the headline grabs. Robbie Fowler signed as a player on 11 July 2011 and, even during the cliched scarf-waving introduction, it was clear that Calisto was not happy. The management (especially the Liverpool-obsessed managing director) had waved through Robbie's spare kilos and his honest assessment during the medical of injuries he had picked up over his career. I was stunned that they failed to at least pause to consider the state of Robbie's body in a country where the wilting heat and stunning humidity would cruelly expose any spare timber being lugged around the pitch. But stars were reflected in eyes and Fowler became the player who team-mates needed to seek out on the pitch so that headlines could be written and clips cut of a free-scoring legend. Of course, this made the play disjointed and predictable for the opposition, especially as keeping up with an ageing and overweight Fowler, whose love of banana milkshakes in his hotel room was catching up with him, didn't prove too difficult. This may have been the club's view, but it certainly wasn't one shared by Calisto.

Away from the PR spin at the Harrow training sessions, Calisto was getting Robbie to train alone to work on his fitness away from the main squad. That rumbled on for a while before coming to an explosive head. It also happened to be the day that I shepherded my two young sons over and suggested they could ask this legend for his autograph but, just as I looked in his direction, he was nose to nose with his coach and not discussing how his weekend had been. Neither was taking a backward step and this was not a solvable situation. So, based on star power, the highly experienced and tactically intelligent Calisto was sacked on 11 September, despite the club being on a run of 11 undefeated games, and replaced by Robbie Fowler as player-coach. Watching him train and coach at Harrow, it was an unfair position to be put in and the season petered out. They would finish in a distant third place, losing four and drawing one of their last five matches and the highlights reel was shorter than a European Super League putsch for a club coming off the back of two consecutive Thai Premier League titles.

Robbie would be replaced after what the club's Wikipedia page endearingly referred to as a 'neutral termination' and a name familiar to English fans, Slaviša Jokanović, ended the six-month experiment that had done little to enhance the reputation of either party. It was obvious from the first day that Jokanović was made of very different gravy and I always wondered how on earth a coach of his capabilities had found himself washed up in an often dysfunctional South-East Asian league. The Serbian's storied playing career had been followed up by two years as the head coach of Partizan Belgrade. I always used to muse as I saw him sitting and watching the often amateurish oversight in front of him whether he had fired his agent, or simply wanted a working holiday that occupied less than 50 per cent of his skills. He would reset the team from top to bottom with a fierceness that brooked no interference from above (spoiler alert) and the following season would see the club return to the summit of Thai football with a crushing and unbeaten campaign that put 14 points between them and runners-up Chonburi. But, despite there being an option for two further years in his contract, he was invited to leave. I asked the MD why such a perfect, unbeaten season hadn't resulted in more of the same and he told me, with a straight face, that they didn't like the way his team played during their 34-game unbeaten season.

To be fair to the club, that season's AFC Champions League saw bitter rivals Buriram United qualify for the knockout rounds after their runners-up spot in Group E, but Jokanović oversaw a miserable Asian campaign that gathered only a single point. That single success came only two days after he signed for the club, with a 2-2 draw at home to eventual Group F runners-up Jeonbuk Hyundai Motors, thanks to a last-minute equaliser for the Quilins. After that, it was not pleasant viewing for the board, ending a miserable campaign with a goal difference of -13 and scoring only two more goals after that hopeful opening. Finishing the campaign with a single-goal home defeat to the other team who failed to make it through, Urawa Red Diamonds, Slaviša would be sacked a month after the defeat and no amount of league wins could save him. The next coach on the carousel was the highly respected German Winfried Schäfer, but he was only to last for a month when Jamaica offered him a job and he did a legger for a three-year term in paradise. So it was back to René to fight fires for the rest of that year before handing over the reins to former Buriram United coach Scott Cooper.

It would be four years before the club could reclaim the championship as fierce rivals Buriram United scooped a hat-trick of titles, while Muang Thong chopped and changed coaches (five more would come and go before their next, and last, league victory in 2016/17).

21

Working for Thai
League Football

A MONTH after Robbie Fowler left and frustrated
by the club's seeming uncertainty to trust me with
any information, I decided to double moonlight my
Harrow and Muang Thong jobs by joining a group
of westerners putting together a website called Thai
League Football. Determined to make an impression
on the Thai football scene, I found out about an English
language website that had been sharing online content
about the beautiful Thai game as a hobby. I went to
meet them on 18 February 2012 and saw there was a
group of people knowledgeable and passionate about
the game who wrote strong match content. I also saw a
great deal of potential but wanted to take it in a different
direction. I planned to create a professional platform to
attract paying sponsors, players and agents. This was an
approach that was to jar greatly with the original site
owner, but for now, I had momentum. I was really lucky
considering my zero budget to bring in Joseph who was

a professional photographer with his own studio that he would regularly put at our disposal. He also persuaded a web designer to create a much more sophisticated website to help put across the professional approach I was looking to develop. Somehow, he agreed to the same payment structure as Joseph: nothing down and the same amount in weekly instalments. I now had the people and the platform. We would produce high-quality English media using our reporters, all paid a flat fee of sweet FA. Exclusive photos taken pitchside by us with interviews in our studio and around Bangkok would also help us stand out in the marketplace. Now I was ready for the launch.

So on 17 March 2012, at the Sportsman Bar Sukhumvit Soi 22, the world (or at least a dozen of them) was introduced to the latest, greatest development. Thai football's Scottish Cafu, Steve Robb (who was halfway through his two years in the kingdom before heading back home to sign for Brechin City), kindly gave us his Thai Port shirt as a prize, which would be framed and placed at the bar to be a focal point for the foreign Khlong Toey legion to meet pre-match. Singha provided the beer and the opening games of that Thai Premier League season were beamed through 11 big screens around the room after our on-stage promotional pitch. The event would also raise 17,280 baht (just over £400) for the Khlong Toey orphanage. It is fair to say that, by the end of the evening, we were collectively buzzing.

But there was one heart-in-mouth moment. Earlier that day I had written a match report for the game Muang Thong won against Police Tero, a club I described as being supported by 'one man and a dog'. I filed the report, got ready for the evening and thought no more about it. But, just before I was about to address the audience, I got a message via our photographer Joseph. The deeply revered late King of Thailand, Bhumibol Adulyadej, was famous not only for his environmental concerns but for the love of his dog Tong Daeng whom he had rescued as a stray. For some reason, an influential Thai thought that my comment was some sort of tangential snub about His Majesty. This was of course ridiculous, but I had to jump off the stage and edit out the 'offending' reference before returning on-stage with bowels far looser than was good for me.

Two months later we had access to Rio Ferdinand's visit to play at Muang Thong's ground as part of Park Ji-sung's charity exhibition game. Optimistically promoted as 'the Asian Dream Cup', this game was part of the revered former Manchester United player's JS Foundation which aimed to promote Asian players on to the world footballing stage. His team also included legendary Japanese player Hidetoshi Nakata and, after being dropped from England's Euro 2012 squad, Ferdinand was also there to play on 23 May. Our photographer Lillian Suwanrumpha took a series of stylish photos but, again, we were building profile without feeding our bank accounts. Sadly, over a decade on, the JS Foundation website is a tumbleweed platform of empty PR centre, some generic and unfocused text

A special Muang Thong atmosphere

I had to rehydrate in these hot times ...

Messi finishes training

My kids enjoying a special Muang Thong United atmosphere

Playing with AIA CEO Ron

Pushing at an open door

The beer truck

The early days supporting Thai football

The kids looking up to our cheerleader

The kit launch

With Steve Morrow and Robert at Harrow

Karen hosts Women Wear Red

Our 'strategic partnership' with Atletico Madrid

Yokohama

Zesh

Charyl with my son

Harrow headmaster Kevin Riley was a great supporter

Kawin

Noi – the Legend

Pawin

With Rochey hijacking the title winning-party

Talking to myself

Bryan

and no sign of any activity for years. The empty News tab informs us that we are currently reading page one – of one.

A week later, my son was chosen as the match mascot for Muang Thong's game against the superbly named Big Bang Chula United and the heady atmosphere seemed to show that Thai football was, as I would finish each of my Muang Thong United English YouTube videos, 'Ready for ASEAN, ready for the AEC.' It just wasn't ready to pay our bills.

There was a great deal of goodwill coming our way for my decision to take a more professional approach. We were picking up more reporters from the regions to make our coverage less Bangkok-centred and I was plodding the city's pavements looking for sponsors and fresh content. A new business often needs a SWOT analysis. Our strength was being the only provider of English material. Our weakness was that we satisfied the smallest of niche markets. This can also be a strength as the audience for such a small market is often highly loyal and active. But, as I often repeat, monetising this passion was a hurdle we would continually crash against. Local Thai broadcasters and websites could pull in millions of interactions whereas ours would be in the thousands or even hundreds. Our decision to reject clickbait and contrived confrontation also meant that we failed to capture the energy of that race to the bottom where arguments seethe and hatred boils over into hurtful but futile threats. Having standards often comes at a cost. The O of opportunity was the recently formed ASEAN trading bloc with a huge population we thought was ripe for English media. The T of threats also started with a T and would be our biggest bugbear: the Thai FA. My decision to produce our own match photos meant we would need the relevant press passes. Luckily Joseph spoke fluent Thai and was tasked with securing the passes that would (let's not forget) professionally project Thai football to a global audience. But that's not how the Thai FA saw it. Sending Joseph from pillar to post and even hiding in their offices when he came calling, they finally relented when he sat on their only working photocopier and refused to move until they coughed up the relevant press passes. They could see he was serious, relented and we were away.

Technically I was a photographer but, unlike Joseph and Lillian who were professionals, I barely knew one end of the camera from the other. My pass gave me access to make connections with coaches, owners and players pitchside and to build up a profile as the only westerner in the media scrum. As crowds grew, this would have been impossible to develop from the stands. Having said that, I also went through security at an FA Cup Final without my security pass or my camera. As foreigners, we moved to different rules. Security probably didn't know what to do with us and decided that letting us carry on was the best form of action. We once went to the cavernous and imposing home stand at Pathum United armed with an *esky* of sodas, ice and local whiskey. Queuing to get in, the people in front had chosen to bring some water in to cope with the uncovered stand and ferocious heat. They were swiftly told this contraband was unacceptable and had their drink confiscated. Our rehydration solution was met with bemused and amused acceptance as we staggered up to the top of the stand that dominated the local skyline to chug through this local firewater. You have to love Thailand.

So we were now building our base and we also had a competitive advantage over the Thai media. Although technically illegal, as for some reason the Thai Royal Air Force saw it as a threat to security (a small detail), we had a transmitter that would send high-resolution photos directly from our cameras to the site. These were the days when photographers would have to wade through thousands of shots to choose their best during half-time or after the match and then wait for the faltering internet signal being sucked up by competing pressmen to finally download their chosen image. For us, it was just a matter of sending the text across to add to the images and we also had the luxury of being able to suggest certain images to seek out before the game that would complement our reports. This meant we could upload a match report less than five minutes after the game had finished and gave us a compelling unique selling point for our building cohort of followers.

My 'do it once, do it right' philosophy was all about premium quality and with Joseph in our group also gave us access to his photo studio a short walk from the Nana Skytrain station right in the centre of the city. Over the next few years, we would invite several players and coaches to be filmed, but two stuck out as the proudest moments to this day. The first was Welsh/Thai player Mika Chunuonsee. Famous (but annoyed by us repeatedly mentioning it) for playing with Gareth Bale as part of the Welsh under-17 elite squad in Cyprus for a 2006 tournament, we decided the best idea was to completely paint his body in both the Welsh and Thai flags. After several hours and far more money for the artist than we could afford, the photos were stunning. So much so that someone decided to steal the image and transpose their watermark on top of ours. In Thailand, 'copyright' is seen as the right to copy. Then, in another frustrating twist, someone else stole it from thief number one and covered the photo with their own logo. When we contacted them and told them how much time, money and effort we had spent on Mika's shoot, they apologised – to thief number one. The other photoshoot I look back fondly on was of Englishman Lee Tuck. A prolific striker who went on to play in Malaysia, the muscular number nine was the perfect player to be Tuck, Lee Tuck 009. These shoots were a great way to widen our network of contacts in the game, giving us everything we needed. Except money.

As the only one in the group who had left their job to drive this passion project, there needed to be a doubling down in efforts to raise income. I called everyone together to pitch the ideas a year after our launch. It didn't go well. There had always been a different philosophy between the original site owner and myself. The rest of the group and I were determined to monetise our content and could see how important it was. The next stage I wanted to explore was for the site to be a shop window for foreign players. For a monthly fee, they would get a professionally presented set of images they could provide or, for an extra fee, have them taken in our studio. All their career highlights and contact details would also be on show. For me, this was the logical next step, but my opponent was adamantly against it. We locked horns for an hour with the rest of the group averting their eyes and by the end of the feisty get-together, it was clear we would never see things the same way. We narrowly avoided coming to blows and never spoke again. I could see the only way to bring in any income was to work as a media cheerleader for individual clubs. I remain proud of our work and the amazing experiences we went through. The website has now lapsed, but the great memoirs remain.

22

I Wish I Could Be like Roland Linz

DURING THIS time of larger and larger expenses with the same zero income working for Thai League Football and voluntarily for Muang Thong (I would later be paid a small retainer), I happened to get to know one of the Muang Thong players. The reason we got to know each other was that, when I was in the stadium car park coffee shop, the Red Cafe, waiting for training to finish to try and build connections with English-speaking players, Roland would often join me, even when his colleagues were working out. Roland was the classic YouTube highlights reel signing. Football is littered with stories of players tricked by clubs and shady agents (especially in those early unregulated Thai football days) but sometimes there is a player who makes clubs pay for their ineptitude and lack of due diligence by simply doing nothing.

In 2013 I had started talking to this friendly young man wearing a club kit assuming he was a trialist or a player I hadn't met before who was injured. But I was soon to discover that my training session coffee buddy was actually a fully (and lucratively) paid-up member of the squad. This 6ft 1in Austrian striker would go on to play 368 professional league games, but 364 were not on the Muang Thong turf. He had enjoyed an impressive career with 39 caps for Austria, including all three of their Euro 2008 matches. He also had successful spells with the French side Nice, Boavista in Portugal, and Austria Vienna. Now, luckily for Roland, in his 32nd year and looking to have one more adventure, he had invested in a high-production-value highlights reel. To be fair to Thai clubs, they didn't have the financial muscle to invite big- (or medium- or small-) named foreign players for a trial, so they often had to dive in and offer everything, lock stock and barrel. But there were ways for Thai clubs to show more depth to their due diligence and minimise risk. In this case, the club's football director pored over every detail of the stylish career clip – except the date. By the time Roland signed, he had a huge volume of games in his legs and, more importantly, a couple of decades on the clock from his greatest hits. He was also right out of shape.

The mistake the club made was assuming that, if they froze this highly paid export out, he would become disillusioned, bang on office tables and demand a move so they could cut their substantial losses. They hadn't reckoned with this phlegmatic young man bringing in a Thai fortune each month to help him dive deep into every aspect of Thai culture. Roland would eventually put his latte down long enough to play four times for Muang Thong and notch a single goal.

Remarkably, I scored one more than him on the same pitch when playing in a charity match for AIA's CEO Ron van Oijen. Roland told them he was happy for the club to pay out his contract but, until that happened, he was going precisely nowhere, which put the club under pressure as the limit on foreign players meant that Roland was making one of those selections dormant. At the time, there were seven foreigners allowed – five in the squad and three in the starting line-up. With one of those foreign starters needing to be from ASEAN, it gave Roland real bargaining power. Eventually, a deal was struck and Roland agreed to move on to the Portuguese team Belenenses where he made three appearances before hanging up his boots. I couldn't help liking Roland and the way he conducted himself. I'd seen scores of foreign players grow increasingly disillusioned with the poor planning and lack of oversight that often described the clubs, but he just sailed through it all happy in the knowledge that his ultimate revenge came every month in the form of a substantial bank deposit with his name on it that, if it didn't appear, he could call on FIFA to investigate. For all their faults, whenever I came across clubs that tried to stiff players and coaches, FIFA showed a robust and supportive response. Even a stopped clock can be right twice a day.

23

The World's Shortest-Running TV Football Show

IN MARCH 2012 I had just quit my secure and lucrative career to carve out a place in the small but rapidly expanding Thai football world. I'd already got to know the Welsh/Thai player Mika Chunuonsee and we got on well. So, I decided we would make the ideal TV team. His attractive athletic looks and my, eh, punctuality. Mika was keen on the idea too, so the next step was to source a production company. We arranged a meeting and both spoke with the Australian owner. Although I had carefully planned our pitch and felt I was explaining the concept, the middle-aged Aussie woman was more interested in Mika's striking good looks. I could have shared the presentation in Serbo-Croatian for all she cared and we still would have received a warm response.

This was easy. They lent us a camera and cameraman to interview one of our friends, Teeratep Winothai (who was still playing in Thai football's top league at the age of 38, until his retirement in November 2022), on the Muang Thong pitch just after his club at the time, Bangkok Glass, had drawn 2-2 on 28 March. We knew him as Leesaw and he was gracious with his time as well as an excellent English speaker after his education at Essex's prestigious private school Brentwood and spending four years with Crystal Palace's youth academy. The interview went well and we passed the production company quality threshold. We had access, contacts and the ability to deliver. The final step was to secure a platform for our show that I decided would be called Total Thai Football. The concept would be part *Soccer AM*, part *Final Score* with a carousel of English-speaking players, coaches and fans joining us both (when Mika's schedule allowed it) or a guest presenter when he had training or a match. I unearthed the original pitch for the show and it certainly didn't lack ambition:

'The style of TTF will be relaxed but informative, thought-provoking but respectful. We will take the pulse of Thai football and give our viewers a glimpse of what it's like behind the glamour and fame enjoyed by the top players. We have access to every facet of Thai football. Some of it will surprise you, some will inspire you. Join us as we lift the lid on the beautiful game in Amazing Thailand.'

Not for us organic and slow growth, but straight into high-production values and meaningful reach. At the time there was an ASEAN television channel in English based in Bangkok called the Thai-ASEAN

News Network. The eloquent and elegant main presenter was also very professional but was having to water down crumbs of content across long segments of sponsored airtime. There was also virtually no sports coverage and definitely no Thai football, so I felt this was our target with the most potential. It seemed a simple case of supply and demand.

Born of the naivety that can only come from someone new to Thai football, I marched over to their headquarters and somehow got a meeting with their anchorwoman. After an impassioned pitch (I had to work harder this time without Mika as eye candy), she seemed to be open to working together. After discussions with her staff, we were told that each episode would only bring in about 40,000 baht (around £1,000). Now, in my heady excitement, I assumed that this was what they would pay us. I couldn't have been more wrong. Let me tell you more.

Now everything was in place. Thai football just needed someone like me to come along with a fresh perspective and a determination to succeed. Yes. I really was that naive. The first piece of career Jenga to be yanked out of my ambitious strategy tower was that, a few days after my meeting, the entire TV company was closed down. Just as my tower started to wobble, the Australian production company owner clarified that the payment for each episode was not to us, but from us. We would be required to commit to a series of shows to make it worth their while and as I, at that point, didn't know any of the movers and shakers who could help sponsor us, our grand project saw less movement than a League Two centre-forward. Understandably, Mika had to focus on his playing career which was to go from strength to strength. By the end of the 2021/22 Thai season, he had won seven Thai caps and was in his ninth season at Bangkok United where he had played more than 150 times and counting. This was another project where timing was everything and, at that point commanding a zero budget, the costs were fatal when, a year or two later, I could have found the funds and influential people to make it happen. Instead, it was to be the first of many body blows when trying to generate any kind of blip on the Thai footballing radar that faded to nothing. We had tried to run before we could walk but looking back through the years I don't regret it. We failed hard and would continue to do so, but it was from a good place with positive intentions.

24

How Not to Be an Agent

SO THERE I was in 2013 continuing to build my profile in Thai football without feeding my bank balance. Needing to change the situation, I decided to turn my hand to being an agent. In my time in the game over there I had seen some heartbreaking stories where busloads of players flown in from Africa would be driven to a range of clubs that would keep the ones they wanted before putting the rejected ones back on the bus and who, if they didn't secure any of the clubs, would be put back on the plane and sent home. There were also foreign players being required to sign contracts written in Thai that left them vulnerable and, when they tried to contact their agent, the SIM card had been changed as soon as the payments had been made. So I decided I would try my hand at being an agent. The plan was (always the start of a sentence that ended badly in Thai football) to be a different type of agent, one that would focus on nurturing and protecting the careers of foreign players. Someone who would act as much as a mentor as a double-dipping intermediary (lots of agents would demand a fee from the club and then a percentage, or all, of the player's signing-on fee before disappearing into the night).

So I decided to work with an Englishman recently coming to the end of his Thai Premier League career and, as a way of staying in Thailand, was also looking to become an agent. He had recent experience and I had a growing list of contacts at the management level. We got on and trusted each other, so decided to try our hand. Our first target was a former Manchester United and Aston Villa youth player who was looking to forge a career in Australia, but we had different ideas. My partner already had a relationship with the player's family and I had identified a club that would give him a trial. So far so good. But then things started to get complicated.

When stopping off in Bangkok on the way over to Australia, we managed to persuade him to leave the airport and make the 100km journey to the club I had arranged his trial at. How on earth he agreed to it all beggars belief. By the end of that evening, he had signed a contract with the club and we had received a fee, in cash, of around £20,000. Not bad for our first day's work and hopefully the start of plenty more projects working together. I found out about the payment as I was making my way into the city centre the next morning to meet my friend Pascal for coffee. A ping on my phone was from a photo of my partner's bed covered in 1,000 baht notes. A man of his word, he gave me my half and I went off to meet Pascal with a spring in my step. I remember being about to reach the Amazon Coffee shop when the phone rang again. It was him with a stark statement, 'You haven't spent that ten grand, have you?' Incredibly, despite seeing him train, knowing his career and signing a contract, the club decided that, at 5ft 6in, the player wasn't tall enough. Now everything we had done came crashing down on us. Our first decision was to return all our fees to the player after we had persuaded him to abandon a career in the A-League. I will always remember the heartbreak of having to visit my local ATM multiple times as there was a withdrawal limit to kill my account balance through death by a thousand cuts, but we both knew it was the right thing to do. The next job was to find him another club. Luckily, a friend of mine agreed to give him a full month's trial which gave us some breathing space and thankfully he went on to sign for them and stay for the whole season, playing the majority of their games. We had learned a valuable lesson. If you want to be a successful agent and be honest, 50 per cent of your plan needs changing.

25

Man in Black

IN JUNE 2014 and the club I was working for had signed a new coach to take over from the much-missed current Thai national coach Alexandré 'Mano' Pölking. As his replacement was flying into Bangkok, I volunteered to pick him up at the airport and take him to his hotel. Arriving at the airport, my wife and I looked askance, as this man dressed head to toe in black scowled across at us. He gave the impression of a man who could start a fight in an empty room and, as the five months of his tenure proved, he was happy to do just that at any imagined provocation.

We took this soon-to-be-signed (and, this being Thailand, soon-to-be-sacked) foreign coach and his assistant out for lunch, welcoming them to the frantic conveyor belt and sending them closer to the boiling coaches' cauldron of the Thai Premier League. Under strict instructions from the more astute 80 per cent of our union, I bit my lip as they set out their dynamic manifesto. They would blitz the club and players with intensive and highly focused training, a new regime of organisation and a far stricter system of accountability and transparency. By the end of the meal, my nails were embedded into my wooden chair frame; the still smoking hole in the side of my head from my wife's laser Stare of Silence smouldered unnoticed.

When I thought it couldn't get worse, they manoeuvred the noose nearer their necks after being introduced in the changing rooms after the previous coach's last game. Some players are family men, some are playboys and many fall somewhere in between, but to tell all of them you know they go to Sukhumvit bars for beer and girls was ill-advised. To then name one road (number 11) as being the place you know they frequent and for your assistant to happily Facebook post from there the following weekend shows the kind of judgement EPL television pundits make choosing meat and potato-hugging trousers with legs splayed for maximum HD effect.

Then, the ISIS School of Public Relations gathered all the backroom staff together to say, in English, that everything was about to change. Most of the staff didn't understand the comments, and those who did were unsure of the message and too nervous to ask for clarification. The particular rancid cherry on the cowpat cake was positioned by another Facebook post showing both men marching aggressively towards the referee to show the importance of 'intensity'. Very classy and backed up by a religion-soaked Twitter campaign that questioned the loyalty of players and resembled a man sawing off a gangplank while kneeling on the seaward side.

Thai life and Thai football are rare breeds indeed. While face-saving and conflict avoidance is not unique in Asia, Thai footballers rarely choose to explore the footballing world to test themselves in the global community. Thai legend Teerasel Dangda was a sacrificial lamb destined to return to Thailand with what was left of his tail firmly placed between his legs once the PR storm abated (the Spanish club Almeria's Thailand cash drop suggested they wanted that done in short order). The fate of 'The Manchester City Three' in 2007, also including Teeratep Winothai at the Crystal Palace and Everton academies and former national coach Kiatisuk 'Zico' Senamuang at mighty Huddersfield Town, added up to a single bagel of first-team appearances. So you have a system which is skewed (rightly, but too strongly) towards native players and only two transfer windows a year when they can be moved on to another Thai club where they continue to influence the players left behind. It's an environment where coaches are completely vulnerable: win, lose or draw. This gives players huge power over their 'boss' and means coaches need to tread on eggshells, not plant landmines in front of them. More importantly, they need to pick their battles.

René Desaeyere had the right approach. Although a fearsome competitor (the image of him fighting, at 63, trying to break through a riot shield against Chonburi still makes me smile), he knew that each player had different buttons to be pressed or avoided. The touchline was his place of pure ferocity where any opposition was fair game, but it invited lazy thinking by the opposition who saw him only as an attack dog. The real battle had already been won: getting the alpha Thai players onside. Foreign players were far easier: shape up or ship out. From who roomed with who, to identifying the strong personalities and giving them extra attention, he didn't make the mistake of arriving like a steamroller to flatten the wheat with the chaff: he listened carefully and learned fast. He quickly saw that, while not club captain at the time, Datsakorn Thonglao was a highly influential dressing-room figure so, in team breakfasts at the Amari Airport Hotel, he would give him high-profile time and attention. He also knew that, while shy, goalkeeper Kawin Thamsatchanan was a model professional who just needed to know the coach believed in him. In the quarter-final of the 2010 AFC Cup first leg against Syrian team Al-Karamah, for the only time, René walked on to the pitch during warm-ups and did some practice with his young keeper to show that he was (literally) right behind him.

Talking with Dick Advocaat when his PSV team visited Thailand in January 2013, the first question he asked about any of the highly skilled Thai players was how hard they trained. We watched the brutally intense session by his players on the Muang Thong pitch on 7 January and his assumption was of a similar level of ferocity for their Thai opponents the following day. When Thai coaches talked about their players' love of 'monkey' games that involve them rolling around the floor, he swiftly disengaged, realising there was little common ground.

In the west it's brutally obvious when you have lost the dressing room but, in Thailand, players rarely seek out conflict. Rather, they will pick up mystery injuries just before a match, play five per cent below their best or get themselves sent off just before a game you can't afford to lose. The rebels in Thailand don't step forward, but everyone takes one step back, leaving the foreign coach a dead man walking. Whether right or wrong, it is a fact of Thai football life. Until coaches seek out good advice from the mass of former foreign coaches before arriving, they will quickly make their first and last mistakes. Just look at René: he got it right at Muang Thong and still got sacked. Twice.

Ominously for the Man in Black (and anyone near him), his first four games ended in defeat as he tried to impose his style on players who universally missed Pölking and couldn't understand why he had left. The rest of the season kept being punctuated by losses after a couple of victories and there was a sense of missed opportunities with the players available, particularly the foreigners who had come for Mano and had stayed to see what would happen next. To be fair to the belligerent Bulgarian mentioned back in chapter 16, his training-ground presence was impressive. He worked the players hard and had a tactically sound knowledge of the game. But this was only on view to a few of us at the enclosed and luxurious training centre. The rest saw a scowling, Brylcreem-haired one-man wrecking ball barging his way through life in a country where social interaction is based on respect and compliance. It was never going to end well.

The coach's and his equally incendiary assistant's final game was a 1-0 win against Jason (son of Peter) Withe's Songkhla United on 2 November, which meant we had finished in a slightly disappointing but not disastrous sixth. But that's not how he and his henchman saw it. Feeling slighted by the tone I had shown in my previous official club social media posting (bizarrely, as it was always the standard asinine positive spin), when we walked over to the massed bank of fans to thank them for their support, the assistant caught up to me as I walked across the centre circle and tried to floor me with a poorly timed right hook. Stunned, but still upright, I demanded to know why he had done that and he proceeded to scream that I had undermined their profile with my comments and how I was working against him. That was nonsense and even more bizarre given that in the last nine games they had only lost twice. His anger seemed to dissipate and I congratulated myself on not returning fire (at the time I was regularly in boxing training). I always had great respect for the club president and felt by sparking out his assistant manager, I would be letting him down. So I left them to their looney conspiracy theories as I congratulated the players and applauded the fans. I thought that would be the end of it but, when I went back to the changing rooms to chat with the staff, the glass door to the shower room had been smashed and our combative assistant was being put into an ambulance after slamming his fist through it. As the ambulance slowly made its way out of the stadium, I knew that would be the last I would see of either of them and I was extremely happy at the prospect.

26

Paul Parker Killed My Career

IN FEBRUARY 2015 I had finally made it (part ten). After years of struggle to promote my speciality product in the mini-market of English content about Thai football, I had been asked on to the regional magazine show *Fox Sports Central* twice in the last week. The feedback from both shows was positive and I'd struck up a strong rapport with Fox's affable host, Steve Dawson. The first appearance was especially memorable. Steve had called me in my nerve centre/ studio/spare room and, while we were chatting away, I heard a countdown from five in the background. Seconds later I was introduced as being one of 'two experts on local football in our midsts' and saw my face beamed up on the studio's big screen. Thanks to Steve's likeable and calm persona, the show went well. Producers from Fox were then in touch to tell me I would need to be a contracted member of the team going forward and they would start to prepare the paperwork and send it from Singapore over to my base in Bangkok.

It also had an extremely positive effect on my profile in the Thai game as opposing players and staff who had seen me on the show now saw me as someone worth talking to and it was also a vindication of the trust my president Varawut Silpa-archa had placed in me. Little did I know that the contract would take over a year to arrive and, thanks to former Manchester United and England legend Paul Parker, this would be the first, and one of the last, times I would ever appear on the show.

But there was still some good news to buoy me up. The next appearance seemed to show my increasing ability to open doors and get interesting content. Bangkok Glass made it to the AFC Champions League qualifying round and were drawn against Malaysian champions Johor Darul Ta'zim (known as JDT) on 10 February. Contacting the club's chairman Pawin before the game, I managed to give Fox Sports cameras access to the game, exclusive interviews with him and affable Aussie player Matt Smith (now newly installed as their latest coach) by Fox reporter Dan Ogunshakin (much to the annoyance of the local Thai media) and a highlights package for the show covering all three Thai goals scored without reply. All these years later, it's heartening to see that Dan has moved from Singapore to Manchester and is now carving out a successful career with the BBC. The whole event and the way it was showcased on *Fox Sports Central* seemed a clear case study for how other Thai clubs could promote their product to a wider audience across Asia. With cooperation and goodwill (don't get ahead of me), Thai football could be a major export. But I was soon to discover that, after this neat and professional showcase for Thai football, what I would receive from most Thai clubs was bewilderment, resentment and obstruction.

I had developed a pre-show routine over the previous shows. Steve would send me the questions he wanted to touch on earlier in the day. I would start by researching the key points I aimed to develop and try (fairly) subtly to produce place names of players I worked with like Charyl Chappuis into my answers. I also made sure I had my Suphanburi FC club shirt ready for product placement by the club sponsors. President Top was paying my wages after all. Once the research was complete, I would walk around our 'high so' local housing estate known as Hyde Park, silently mouthing the key points I wanted to hit (probably looking like a man two thirds of a bottle into the deadly Samsong local whiskey to the wealthy residents) and working out how I could give Steve the best insight into the world of Thai football. Then it was back to check the *Bangkok Post* to see if its forthright sports writer Tor Chittinand had any insights on the latest story and I was pretty much set. The final job was to put Post-its with the key stats around the screen of my computer ready to drop into my Skype report and I was good to go.

But this time, things were different. Usually, we would film in the mid-afternoon so they had time to edit the content and check for timing. But the usual deadline came and went as I sat in my spare room going through my lines and coaching myself about keeping my head still with a well-modulated voice that didn't spin off into the cadences of local radio DJs. Later, much later and just before going on air, I had a message from the producer telling me that everything was pushed back as the previous guest, Paul Parker, had turned up late, delaying everything else. This didn't seem to be a problem at the time. The editing team seemed rushed and stressed, but that was understandable with such a short deadline looming before the evening show. Anyway, I was prepared. Steve was the consummate professional, I knew his questions and was ready with my responses. What could possibly go wrong?

Usually, we would go through everything before going on air, checking levels and the quality of the online connection. This time, the producer went through the problems of time with me and how we needed to crack on. The team in the editing booth were nervous but friendly and all desperate to get this segment done, so we dived in. I mentioned that I couldn't hear Steve in the studio, but their increasing stress levels seemed to be focusing their minds less on getting this segment right and more on editing the clickbait content of Parker so that he came across well and would maybe recommend the show to some of his former Red Devils team-mates.

When the show started, I had a crystal-clear connection with everyone in the sound booth. In my ear mic, I could hear all the stories of their weekend and what they needed to do to polish that day's show. The only problem was that Steve's voice was like listening to someone on the other side of a busy party. Cutting through the immediate noise was unnerving because, like listening to a conversation from your mother-in-law when the football is on, you think you can block out the immediate content and concentrate on the one that matters, but her tones are troublingly familiar and constantly trick your brain into focusing on her banal ramblings about her unhelpful neighbours and their hedge-clipping habits.

I decided to try and style the interview out by answering the questions I had been given earlier and hoping Steve had asked them, then trying desperately to filter out any follow-up questions from the editing-booth banter pouring into my ears in high definition. The result wasn't pretty. Looking back on the video, one of the questions I guessed wrongly and then, when I started to suspect what I had done, I cocked my ear to the screen like a Victorian pensioner in need of an ear trumpet. The look in my eyes was less rabbit in a headlight and more rabbit in a bear trap with Farmer Palmer calmly cocking his shotgun nearby.

The show went out and, watching my segment through plaited fingers, I knew they had needed to try and edit any salvageable content from me into something less like a televisual car crash. Exactly the last thing they needed on a day like that, with the Parker content still not ready. And like that, the phone and emails fell silent. All communication was now one way; from me to them. Bizarrely, a year later I received

187

a seven-page contract from Fox Sports to employ me as a commentator. As far as I know, a copy of it still sits in the safe at Suphanburi FC after I gave it to the president, thinking forlornly that this would propel me back into the *Fox Sports Central* orbit.

27

My Thai Football Soulmate:
René Desaeyere

THE CHRONIC insecurity felt by foreign players and coaches in Thai football, particularly in the Wild West early years, meant working days were overshadowed by nervous glances over their shoulders for a potential replacement. I even knew of a large Thai Premier League club that brought in a coach's replacement unannounced to join a training session before relieving the incumbent of his duties. Ironically, they were so keen to get him into the hot seat that they didn't do due diligence on his CV and it soon came to light that much of it was untrue. This understandable paranoia also affected the way they dealt with me. Phone messages would come in three distinct stages:

> Stage 1: Hi Matt. How are you doing? (the setup)
> Stage 2: How is the family? (the icebreaker)
> Stage 3: Have you got the number for [insert name here?] (the money shot)

At the time, I would bristle at this tactic and the predictable staccato structure I pointed out in real-time to my wife. But now, with the perspective of time and experience, I can see that hustling was the only way to be one step ahead of the shove to the exit door. As oceans of money started to flood into Thai football, agents circled and noticed that I had a fertile phone list. Many of these 'agents' were unlicensed and unregulated by a governing body barely able to agree on the day of the week. I would be lunched and gently prodded for introductions and connections to key movers and shakers. They were much easier to repel. As a father to two sons, all I needed to do was ask myself if this was the type of person I wanted to influence my boys and 11 times out of ten the answer would be 'no'. The only exception would be with the former player I mentioned in the chapter 'How Not to Be an Agent', so you can tell from that title how well it went. Into this Thai woozy world of whispers and back-channelling stepped in yet another coach for serial sackers Muang Thong United. After a run of three Thai coaches, club shareholder and aspiring football mogul Robert Procureur seemed to be consolidating his power base with the signing of his friend René Desaeyere. I went to yet another press conference assuming this new appointee was one more stooge for the man behind the man approach often used in Thailand when the man (it was always men) you don't see is the one who has the real power. In politics it was known as 'the third hand': an ominous and slightly bizarre image to describe where the real power source would often lie. But I was about to be very pleasantly surprised.

René had a long playing career that ended in 1987, with the most noticeable period being at FC Antwerp where he had played 191 times. But that afternoon in January 2010 he seemed just another passing occupant in the red-hot coaching carousel seat of Muang Thong United. René is an intimidating physical presence. A burly midfielder in his playing days, even at the age of 62 he retained the gait of someone who could handle themselves when required. Remarkably he had already been coaching for a quarter of a century at a startling 16 different clubs. His most high-profile success was in 2000 at Cerezo Osaka when they won 66 per cent of their games and he was voted Coach of the Year in Japan. René would go on to coach an eye-watering total of 23 clubs and when I spoke to him recently he was set fair, at the age of 74, in the beautiful Thai coastal resort of Hua Hin. That is the real measure of the man and his passion for this sport.

There was a long-running story between us that René had been part of the Antwerp team that beat my family's Aston Villa in the 1970s. I was so used to coaches arriving and spouting claims that rarely stood up to scrutiny that I assumed it was just another smokescreen to hide how he had arrived in this relative footballing backwater. The iPhone had only arrived recently in Thailand when he first told me, so this story, like many others, was shared in late-night bars and would be half-remembered the following morning when firing up a squat and slow desktop. The story ran for so long because, unlike now, we were less infatuated with instant fact-finding rather than letting a story grow organically. Now all narratives have to be trounced into dull certainty in less than a googling second in case they are given room to breathe.

Bizarrely, watching the Women's Euros in July 2022 I saw Louis van Gaal at Sweden v the Netherlands which reminded me of the tall tale, so I decided to search for 'Van Gaal Antwerp'. Even more strangely, the only image that came up on the photo site was Aston Villa's programme cover for their UEFA Cup first-round second-leg defeat to the Belgians on 1 October 1975, which he played in. I sent the image to René in Thailand and he called me back later the same day. By another remarkable coincidence, just before heading back to the kingdom, René was interviewed for a documentary on Van Gaal that came out just before the Qatar World Cup, discussing how he had taken the then 20-year-old under his wing as René had a Dutch wife who could help Louis settle into life in Antwerp. But even at such an early age, Van Gaal's infamous abrasiveness was forming. Describing how, because she had used milk instead of cream, the coffee she had offered him 'looked like pee', he was not welcome into the Desaeyere home again.

For the Villa games, René was banned for picking up a red card against Van Gaal's former club Ajax in the previous season's competition and, although some of the players were carrying injuries and the

Meeting Robbo

Robbo at Harrow

Robbo touring Harrow

There's cake and then there's CAKE

Chutinant 'Nick' Bhirombhakdi

*Interviewing Mr
Singha Corporation*

*The King of Buriram
will see you now*

The King of Buriram

Suphanburi fans were immense that season

A night out with John Barnes

Lee's too Sharpe for me

The Harrow All Stars

Embarrassment of riches

Thai Tiger King

Teaching football English

All aboard the Thai Football Tours

Spreading the word

Thai Port fans are immense ...

The final football sunset

The glamorous life ...

Wish you were here?

Belgians couldn't even field a full bench, the first-leg 4-1 win was added to at Villa Park by a single-goal victory. Van Gaal was a fringe player partly because, unlike now, Belgium had a tight rule that only three foreigners could be selected and they already had three established internationals, so the Dutchman was often left kicking his heels waiting for infrequent opportunities. Ironically, this frustrating playing situation gave Van Gaal time to watch the academy training and find out who showed the most promise. This would help launch his coaching career after retiring a decade after the Villa game where three roles in Ajax as youth coach, assistant and head coach honed the skills he would take to Barcelona in 1997 for three storied (and confrontational) successful seasons.

So, going back to that press conference in 2010, the moment René walked in, he owned the room. There would always be a feeling when he was talking that you were trying to control a silverback gorilla with a fly swat. There was a thin veneer of control, but when the chest-thumping started, you were going wherever he took you. We hit it off immediately. I have always believed that, when you are dealing with a hurricane, the safest place to be is in the centre of it. You can see the carnage and chaos all around you, but your position is eerily calm. I knew Robert passingly well at the time. So the three of us went out after the pitchside photos for an exploration of Bangkok. Fast forward and over 'Jack and Coke' at three in the morning, we felt we had known each other for years.

The key part of our friendship was trust. Secrets would be kept without discretion needing to be asked for and, unfashionably in football and life in Thailand, we would always arrive on time for any arranged meet-up. We shared annoyance at people turning up late, something that came across as bizarre to club colleagues, but René's steaming responses to being left to wait around soon got the message out loud and clear that the concept of 'on time' was not based on hierarchy or negotiation. He even disciplined club and national legend Teerasil Dangda for assuming that, because he was injured, he could help his sister move house instead of doing rehab. A mistake he only made once.

The home fans also took to him immediately while the away support often vilified him for his attack dog approach on the touchline. I remember when, as BEC-Tero coach against Muang Thong, he felt the opposition (and now head coach) player Mario Gjurovski had dived. He went nose to nose with the man 40 years his junior and had to be separated by the coaching staff. Mario's shock at that moment was only compounded a few months later when René would become his new boss.

On paper, a coach with two dozen clubs looks like a man who was impossible to work with. In reality, René had the passionate support of two sides of the footballing triangle. The fans loved him and the players worked for him. I could always tell when the Muang Thong training sessions were on at the Harrow pitches as I made my way back from work. I could hear René barking instructions during small-sided games in ways I had never heard in training sessions at other clubs. But the last corner of the triangle was often René's downfall. He didn't kowtow to interference from people who knew nothing about the game. Instructions from meddling senior management to select players not knowing they were unavailable or had trained poorly during the week were flatly ignored. It was his way or the highway, and not even winning the Thai Premier League title would make it his way.

Rather like with me, Thai clubs didn't seem to know what to do with René. They could see his credentials as a coach and tactician. They warmed to his alpha-male personality, but the deferential, hierarchical structure of Thai society simply couldn't cope with this rampaging figure bursting through gatekeepers of social conventions. It took someone with a different approach to see his qualities more clearly. Just before flying north to discuss terms with Chiang Mai FC, we had the kind of flirtatious but ultimately fruitless meeting with a club then known as Bangkok Glass (now BG Pathum United) that calls on huge resources from the Singha Corporation through chairman Pawin Bhirombhakdi's family.

Before the meeting, we got together in a nearby hotel to discuss what we wanted from the club and how we would navigate the hours ahead to ensure there was the right outcome without alerting anyone to our presence there. Football is a strange world of oversharing interspersed with cloak-and-dagger secrecy.

We knew that this was the time for the latter and any attempt at the former would doom the afternoon to be a wasted one. We also knew the club shared our approach because, instead of meeting at their imposing Leo stadium, we were called to their offices just down from the traffic vortex of hell that is Asoke junction. Over the next two hours, we danced around the Thai elephant in the room that René was available and ready for work with the plan that I would be his director of football but, for whatever reason, Pawin didn't pull the trigger and we left feeling this was as much a tyre-kicking exercise as a process put in place to make us an offer. The questions seemed to have an unspoken undersong. It felt to me like they were centred on René's Muang Thong United connections. Would he return there? Did they have plans for him? These questions seemed to cause Pawin uncertainty and ultimately the meeting ended in the kind of huge positivity that you know will lead to nothing.

René's Thai career was to drift to a disappointing end, with spells at BEC-Tero and a second brief encounter at Muang Thong. This was a sliding-doors moment when a club rich in resources but crying out for a galvanising presence like René would continue to follow the law of diminishing returns until Bangkok Glass's relegation in 2018. As I play that meeting over in my head, I wonder what I could have said to have sealed the deal. Maybe, after two hours of sharing the room with René, Pawin decided that the centre of a hurricane was not the place for him.

28

Thailand: Where Trash-Talking Comes as Standard

IN ENGLISH football, mumbled press conference platitudes bleat, 'They are an excellent team so we need to play our best. We know how dangerous Hartlepool can be, so even though we are in the EPL we expect a really tough game.' In Thailand, things are just a little different. Over the years I have sat through dozens of Thai pre-match press conferences astonished at the words I hear. Like the laughable invitation to Uruguay for a friendly, Thai clubs will often announce invitations and signings as done deals before redacting history once the inbox falls silent. In the west, coaches would be pilloried post-match for their outlandish predictions and lack of respect for the opposition, but in Thailand, the need to save face means crazy pre-match claims tend not to be referred back to. Coaches will reveal formations, player injuries and predictions for the final score. Seemingly paradoxically in the kingdom where respect is seen as a key societal plank, coaches will often boldly state that they are the better team and a win is expected.

Notoriously, while I was working for Suphanburi FC, the precursor to the SCG Muang Thong United match with us saw the home side's official media bark out that their opposition was 'not in our class'. This proved to be correct, but they needed to look higher rather than lower in the class rank to find their opponents who romped to a 5-2 victory. In England, this would have caused huge resentment and anger, but here it was only us expats who got hot under the collar. The *jai yen yen* approach of Thais where extremes of emotion are shied away from meant that, after a stadium-based party at the end of the game, a neutral onlooker watching Suphanburi fans file out of the SCG Stadium would have been unsure who won and who just suffered their worst-ever defeat.

What disorientates westerners is that these statements aren't delivered like boxers desperately drumming up ticket sales with outlandish threats and promises of war but, like many seemingly contradictory aspects of living in Thailand, the comments are offered as statements before the fact. Former Thai national coach Kiatisuk Senamuang started with a straight bat before going for that six over cow corner when he shared how: 'Their players are good technically and we cannot underestimate them. But many of them are slow and past their prime.'

Even by the normal standards of breathtaking directness, this is bold. Seemingly a quote to be pinned to the opponent's dressing-room wall as inspiration or disrespectful to the highest-ranking FIFA team in ASEAN, the day's Thai papers simply carried it neutrally and as a matter of obvious fact. In the end, the War Elephants would beat the Philippines over the two-legged round and win the final against Malaysia three days later, so maybe he knew what he was doing.

East or west, which is best? Snore-fest or startling honesty? Give me an outrageously direct Thai pre-match where cards are not held close to the chest but scattered across the floor any day.

29

Teaching English to Thai Players

EVER DETERMINED, one of my many enthusiastic but hair-brained schemes was to prepare a curriculum to teach English to Thai footballers as a way of helping to develop their careers and spread the word about Thai football right across ASEAN. What could possibly go wrong? So: I could tell there was a gap in this market. Noticing how many Thai players spoke no more than a basic functional level of English, I came up with a cunning plan. Why not create a teaching programme specifically aimed at the challenges Thai speakers had with speaking English? All I needed to do was create the curriculum, promote the philosophy behind it and we would be off and running. What could be simpler? So here was the spiel:

Suphanburi FC's SMART Football English Programme
  'See
  'Move
  'Apply
  'Repeat
  'Think'

I even managed to persuade Bryan Robson to write the foreword below while he was the Thai national coach:

'In my Manchester United playing career, foreign team-mates were the exception rather than the rule (unless we include the Scottish lads!). My Red Devils league debut against Manchester City on 10 October 1981 was as part of a 22-man squad containing 11 English, five Scottish, four Irish and one Welsh player. The only foreigner was Holland's sublimely skilled Arnold Muhren. By the time of my last United appearance on 8 May 1994, young English players like David Beckham and Paul Scholes were joined by Ukrainian Andrei Kanchelskis, Frenchman Eric Cantona and Dane Peter Schmeichel but these were the only foreigners in my final Manchester United squad and they all spoke English at least adequately. The birth of the English Premier League two years beforehand was starting to globalise the game and now, 23 years later, the United squad looks very different indeed. With only 11 of the 23-man squad being English and no other British representatives apart from the legendary Ryan Giggs on the coaching bench, football truly has become a League of Nations.

'In September 2009 I became Thailand's national coach and it was here I saw first hand the importance of a common language. Thailand has strict restrictions on non-Thai players with a team only allowed three foreign and one foreign Asian player. They are also restricted to five foreigners in a squad. In coaching sessions, I was lucky to have fluent English-speaking Thai players Leesaw and Rangsan who grew up in England but, generally, for a group of international players, their English was poor and it made getting the message across during training quite a challenge for me and my assistant, Steve Darby.

'Now in my role as Manchester United global ambassador, I regularly see the importance of universal communication. Football is a fantastic tool for teaching language that can combine the players' passion for the game with their need to be understood quickly and accurately. Learning language can also take place on the training ground just as easily as in the classroom and create a sense of unity, purpose and team spirit that can only be good for the beautiful game.'

I followed it up with an impassioned call to arms that I was convinced would get people's attention and bring them flocking to this innovative new system, 'Speaking English is more than "knowing that."

'Like playing a sport, it is also a physical "knowing how".

'Suphanburi FC's SMART Football English Programme brings structure to passion. Playing the beautiful game in Thailand, especially with four non-

Thai speakers in each team, makes quick and accurate communication vital. A common language of English creates a marginal gain that not only improves player confidence but actively enhances team performance, converting to more points, higher league positions and cup success.

'A Thai goalkeeper with foreign defenders or two midfielders of different nationalities has a split second to share vital information accurately and spontaneously. Physical gestures have limited use and are open to misinterpretation across cultures. They also force players to watch their team-mates instead of their opponents or the ball, creating uncertainty and delay. With clear pronunciation through realistic practice, a constantly expanding range of key football terms creates clarity of communication amidst the confusion and crowd noise of a football match.

'As fans see the way their heroes value and use English, players will become English ambassadors to promote wider use of the language both across the Suphanburi province and among other teams, including the men's and women's national teams. This method is also ideally suited to the young players yet to start their professional careers as we approach the ten country ASEAN bloc opening its doors to six hundred million people using English as the official language.

'Suphanburi FC's SMART Football English Programme deliberately starts with players who have little to no English vocabulary. Through a highly structured and tailored curriculum, these players will be guided from nervous beginners to confident users. There will be some players who choose not to make this journey, but that choice is a chance for the football club to assess their character and motivation to be a high-achieving footballer in a global sporting world.'

And now for the reality:

The key prerequisite for players to make meaningful progress was the consistent practice I had aimed to be built into their daily training routine. I had a lot to learn. The players were keen to give the course a try, but there were two key problems. Firstly, training session locations and times were a moveable feast whose menu I wasn't privy to. Time and again I would turn up to the session to find that either it had happened, wouldn't happen or wouldn't happen there. Such a hit-and-miss approach made progress painful. Rather than moving through the course, I was constantly going back to minute one of lesson one. The second challenge was the seriously mind-bending heat. Either I would be getting the players overheated before training or they were spent and roasting by the time they got to me. Again, a grand plan of mine was about to hit the scorched provincial Thai dust.

The idea was sound in the right environment. An embedded educational programme supported by clubs (especially for academy teams) would create added value for players and give them the incentive to study as part of their professional development.

Unfortunately, there are precious few Thai clubs that apply consistency and continuity. Short-term fixes and trigger-happy owners don't just reduce the power of the players, but lessen the chances of creating anything long-lasting connected to the clubs. Looking back through the wreckage of all that pointless work, I still feel there was merit in it.

This was my course's philosophy:

'Suphanburi FC's SMART Football English Programme helps young players gain competence with confidence. It also gives players opportunities to show leadership and collaboration skills to communicate in English and help them mature as players and individuals. There are 350 core words and phrases that make up the course, but the lessons will become more skill-based as players progress through each level.

'There are three key aspects of the course that make it unique. Firstly, especially in the early stages, lessons will be delivered mirroring training sessions using the Total Physical Response method pioneered by James Asher, a professor of psychology at San José State University. These lessons will not only take place on the training pitch, in the gym and around the training centre, but each lesson will also include aspects of training such as:

'Modelling
'Drills
'Interaction between players, both in groups and pairs

'Physical movement to embed understanding of course content

'The second unique aspect of this course is how much its content is tailored and adapted to the needs of the players. Lessons will take place immediately before training, so meaningful vocabulary can be acquired, mastered and quickly applied in a realistic environment. The instructional vocabulary used in those training sessions will then be identified, grouped into sound categories and taught in future SMART lessons.

'The third unique element of the course is how phonic sounds and blends are taken from the Early Years Foundation Stage of the British National Curriculum, so language acquisition has a strong and tested scaffold where players can focus on individual sounds in each section of a lesson to help develop their confidence, rather than being bombarded with a whole range of previously unknown vowels and consonants.

'Unfortunately, the reality in football is that most young players fail to become professionals. This course, broken down into three overlapping but developmental steps containing 30 lessons in each module, will equip them with a broad base of English skills that can be applied to a range of future scenarios.

'SMART Passers will focus on basic vocabulary development and key English sounds.

'SMART Shooters will access higher level and more conceptual vocabulary, beginning to apply it in a range of communication situations.

'SMART Scorers will be expected to apply vocabulary, grammar and higher-level communication skills in a range of realistic scenarios.

'Each level will be made up of 30 weekly lessons and the course aims to bring a player with no English to fluency over a three-step, 90-lesson process spanning two years.'

I decided to change focus and teamed up with an English programme being delivered in a provincial government school centred on English language acquisition. I built in club visits both for them at the stadium and for the squad to meet them at the school. They wrote English articles for our matchday programme and the strongest students joined me on matchday to meet our VIP guests and sponsors. Having the structure of weekly timetabled lessons gave me a real sense of progress with children highly motivated to improve their English levels, but it still saddened me that, in what should be a similarly regimented world of professional footballers, we couldn't slot in daily or even weekly times to focus on their English acquisition.

30

A Cunning Plan:
Football Tourism

TEACHING MARKETING as part of my day job, I often highlight to my students the importance of 'getting past the no' in general and failure in particular. To illustrate this, I try to apply the Pareto Principle. Put simply, the law argues that for the majority of outcomes, roughly 80 per cent of consequences come from 20 per cent of causes (the 'vital few') which leaves the useless majority clogging up the rest of your time. In true springer spaniel fashion, I decided in 2013 that the province of Suphanburi was just the place for football tourism to take hold. I will leave you to guess on which side of the Pareto ledger this well-intentioned idea was to fall.

With club president Top's connections, I managed to get a puff piece printed in the *Bangkok Post* on 2 March 2013, under the headline 'Suphanburi welcome fans'. It read, 'Suphanburi FC have initiated a project to use football to promote tourism in the province, believed to be the first of its kind in the Thai Premier

League. Suphan Buri province is only an hour's drive from Bangkok, but tourism attention has often been diverted to nearby Kanchanaburi or further afield to the northern cities of Chiang Rai and Chiang Mai. Thai Premier League newcomers Suphanburi FC hope to help shake off the province's image of being a place for a short stay or a stop-over to other destinations. Suphanburi FC president Varawut Silpa-archa explained his plan, "Suphanburi FC will act in accordance with Thailand's national policy on tourism and sports and this is why we have initiated a tourism and sports project."

'"Our club will not only promote the province's tourism among Thai fans but also international visitors. If the project is successful, it should encourage other Thai football clubs, not only those in the top flight, to establish a similar programme. The main aim of the plan is to invite fans of visiting teams, including foreigners, to arrive in the province a few days before their match."

'The fans will meet their Suphanburi FC counterparts, who will help take them to visit the province's famous tourist spots such as the Suphan Buri Tower, Dragon Descendant Museum, Samchuk old market and buffalo show. The visitors may stay at Bueng Chawak, the province's famous home-stay area. This will also help create a friendly rivalry among fans of opposing teams.'

Now for the reality. My long-suffering, football-financing wife reluctantly agreed to join me on her half-term holiday for a fact-finding mission to design a detailed itinerary that would wow the football-fan market. The month before that article came out, Karen was subjected to long treks around a dusty and rarely visited museum, a water park that had closed down but, when finding out who we were visiting on behalf of, was hurriedly opened up for the four of us, and a tree-house holiday park that, while having great views across a lake, seemed to have had no interaction with tourists since time began. With every tedious and dusty lowlight, Karen was becoming more and more frustrated at her planned downtime being hijacked for a trip exploring attractions in need of overhaul or closure. After visiting a zoo that was probably cutting edge in 1972, her patience snapped and she returned to Bangkok, leaving me to be driven from tired pillar to dusty post trying to enthuse hotels with my vision for high-paying tourists who also had high expectations of service and visit that, increasingly obviously, couldn't be catered for.

The one part of the fast-unravelling campaign that stood up to scrutiny was the stadium. It had been greatly modernised and was certainly popular when we could provide behind-the-scenes interactions with players and staff. The training centre a few minutes' drive from there was also highly impressive, modern and purpose-built. The challenge was that both facilities were surrounded by vast tranches of nothingness, so the idea of having several activities throughout the day was floundering as it became increasingly obvious that the infrastructure, English speakers and itineraries were all in need of the kind of improvement that I simply couldn't access. We also had a state-of-the-art team bus that was the last word in luxury and could be used when available to pick tourists up. When Harrow Bangkok came to visit, they were given a tour of this five-star vehicle and it persuaded me this would be the way that tourists could be ferried around. But even this relatively small detail was mired in confusing complexity when it became clear that I would not be given access to its itinerary, accessibility or, often, its location.

So, despite a breezy piece of in-house spin promoting the tourist-focused programme, it faded into obscurity.

Like so many of my projects in Thai football, this was another example of the right idea in the wrong time and place.

31

Goodbye to All That: A Farewell to Thai Football

OVER THE years we had got used to how clubs would help subsidise and even completely cover some of the travel expenses of their fans. Buriram took fan financial support a step further. There were regular rumours in the early days that supporters were paid for transport, food and even medical bills while also being offered free shirts to boost sales figures. It was surprising to see, in such an impoverished region, so many fans wearing brand-new club shirts, but this was a practical and pragmatic move for Newin who had produced a stadium that, when complete, had almost as many seats as the city contained citizens at the time. It's very easy to adopt western scorn toward paying fans, but many of these people lived a money-free life that consisted of subsistence farming and a diet of rice given by family members and fruit from nearby trees.

This feeling of righteous indignation was stoked again in May 2016, two months before my six-year affair with Thai football ended. British journalists poured scorn on the way local people had been paid to cheer Leicester City's open-top bus during their Bangkok victory parade after winning the Premier League. *The Sun* screamed: 'THOUSANDS of Thais were paid to pose as Leicester City fans for the club's Premier League victory parade in Thailand, we can reveal.'

The sea of blue and white scarves and banners were sourced by a social media campaign offering each 'fan' 500 baht (around £11) to be an extra in the Foxes' parade. Each actor was then given a free T-shirt after meeting at King Power's HQ and told to sing for their free supper. British journalists were also clutching their pearls at the fact many of the King Power employees were required to become Leicester supporters for the day, but this is transposing a very different mentality on their actions. When I first went to Muang Thong games, I was impressed that, like Rochey and I, many of the original fans would come to every game, home and away. It wasn't until I worked for the club and went to the owning company Siam Sport's headquarters that I realised this was another exercise in crowdsourcing, and cheering Muang Thong was part of their job description. Maybe because I had lived in the kingdom for so long, I couldn't get hot under the collar about it. Comparing this behaviour with an English team was comparing apples to oranges. English football has a huge history to draw on and most of its citizens have enough disposable income to visit the stadium and pay for the overpriced souvenirs (often made at a small fraction of the price in Thailand). Thai football cannot draw on that history of resources, so a shortcut seems the best way to manufacture an atmosphere rather than have the champions of England enduring a parade of mildly curious shoppers and bored tourists. I had no real problem with it, suggesting I had started to be conditioned into the values of Thailand more than I realised.

So, on 13 July 2016 after an easy 3-0 FA Cup second-round win over lower-league Krung Thonburi, I put down my security lanyard, propped it against a can of Chang and took a photo to say goodbye to Thai football. A month beforehand I had been a speaker at a Sports Management International Conference in Bangkok which, fittingly after my years of banging on about it to anyone who would listen, was attended by delegates from across ASEAN. In my presentation, I reviewed a Powerpoint called 'Rising Asia' which set out the journey I had been on so far in Thai football from supporting my local team to working for them and going on to promote Thai football as a regional brand. It felt like an appropriate swansong given that the SMART Football English Programme, appearances on Fox and work with local teams had all run their course. I was determined to go out with a bang and harangued the ASEAN audience with a passionate invocation of Asia's huge, and largely untapped, footballing potential. I was getting into my stride and felt I had the room enthused when, looking out to the front row, I saw one of the main organisers fast asleep, mouth wide open and snoring. It felt like my Thai football epitaph.

This seemed to be a suitable last hurrah supported by my president and his wife Kay. Six years of trial through error had come to a low-profile end. The season would be another disappointing one with the club continuing their decline and ending up in tenth with Brazilian Márcio Rozário and Spaniard Carmelo González as the last quality foreign players surrounded by increasing levels of mediocrity from home and abroad. Earlier in the year, I had joined René for the final time at Muang Thong where we both said goodbye to the training players and a spectacular sunset greeted us as we looked back on a stadium that held oceans of memories for us both.

32

Time to Pass on the Baton

SO THAT was it. After 16 years in the kingdom with half a dozen of them working in Thai football, it was time to board a one-way flight from Bangkok's Suvarnabhumi Airport for the first time. There were mixed emotions as I checked in. Thai football was in a good place and I now enjoyed a hard-won profile within it. I had cultivated a network of trustworthy, open-minded and helpful contacts in the game that knew I could also be trusted with on and off the record content. But, at the same time, I knew that my nichest of niche markets was unlikely to be sustainable in the long run, so getting out when things were good seemed to have plenty of merit.

What put my mind at ease was how the provision of objective and well-researched content that I hoped I had provided would carry on with my friend Paul 'Scholsey' Murphy. Bearing a striking resemblance to the former Manchester United great, Paul was also a midfield terrier in his playing days. We were opponents, team-mates, colleagues and friends over my time in the kingdom and now he is continuing the coverage of football in the country as well as widening his remit to review football across ASEAN.

Unlike me, Scholsey had a background in journalism, starting his work with British newspapers in 2005 and then, in his second spell, in Thailand (his first one coincided with my arrival in 2000 and lasted for five years). In 2013, he decided to put that experience to use in the Thai beautiful game. Paul also worked with me on the Thai League Football website and, when it lapsed, went on to write several features and match reports for Thai League Central that are still going strong to this day.

I wanted to give you a flavour of Scholsey's work to finish the book and he kindly shared this article with me. It shows that, for all the money now flowing through the Thai game, there remains a reassuring river of beautiful madness too. Enjoy:

'Fans of the *Hangover* films will remember the moment in *Part II*, when having just about given up all hope, the protagonists solve the mystery of their missing friend, Teddy.

'Sitting in a riverside restaurant in Bangkok, a power outage triggers the memory and leads them to their hotel lift, where Teddy was trapped after a power cut the previous day.

'The rather lazy scriptwriting led the audience to believe that such problems with electrical supply were an everyday occurrence in Thailand's capital city. The truth is, they are not, though recent events at the PAT Stadium might lead many to believe that the writers of the second of the *Hangover* films had a point.

'For the second time in three weeks, Port FC saw the lights go out on matchday as they prepared to host Muang Thong United in a keenly anticipated clash. Fans were already milling outside and some were in the stadium when it became apparent that all was not well. Rather than respond with transparency to the emerging problem that appeared to have been caused by the generator – loud bangs had been heard and smoke had been seen – the club decided to pretend that nothing was going on and hoped that some desperate repair work could solve the problem and save face.

'The media who were already in place were not allowed to leave, while no one else was allowed in as security goons patrolled the area behind the main stand, near the alleged offending generator. The goons were also checking the phones of journalists and telling them not to take and share photos of the developing drama. This was shameful treatment of the people there to do a job and did anyone really think that with fans already in the stadium, word would not get out? At one point the security team could be seen forming a human chain in front of the generator as if they were protecting a high value target from a mob of protestors.

'As tension built and nerves frayed, hope gave way to resignation as it became clear the match would not go ahead. After club owner Nualphan Lamsam departed the scene in her Rolls-Royce, the tension evaporated and the crowds trooped home.

'Three weeks ago, the power had failed with just a couple of minutes remaining in Port's home match with Police Tero with the score tied at 1-1. The hosts were forced to forfeit the match and Tero were awarded a 2-0 victory. There were no problems off the pitch the following week, though the 1-0 home defeat to BG Pathum United did lead to the dismissal of head coach Jadet Meelarp.

'On Sunday, Port were hoping for a fifth win in seven league matches against Muang Thong United when the electrics scuppered hopes of lifting fan spirits after a difficult period. Port started the year with big dreams and were considered very much as major title contenders when the season restarted last month. Since then, the club has had more attention than any other for all the wrong reasons. In the midst of a pandemic when most clubs were tightening their belts, Port were splashing the cash to try and bring that coveted T1 title within their grasp.

'But the club with apparently the most to spend cannot keep the electricity in its stadium in working order. Once could be out down to bad luck, but twice in such a short space of time is bringing the game into disrepute.

'In a country where losing face is something to avoid at all costs, Port have embarrassed themselves and all of Thai football with recent bungling. It remains to be seen if the Thai League will take a hard line and award the three points to Muang Thong, or if Port can use force majeure as an explanation and have the match rescheduled.'